STĀN

D1132845

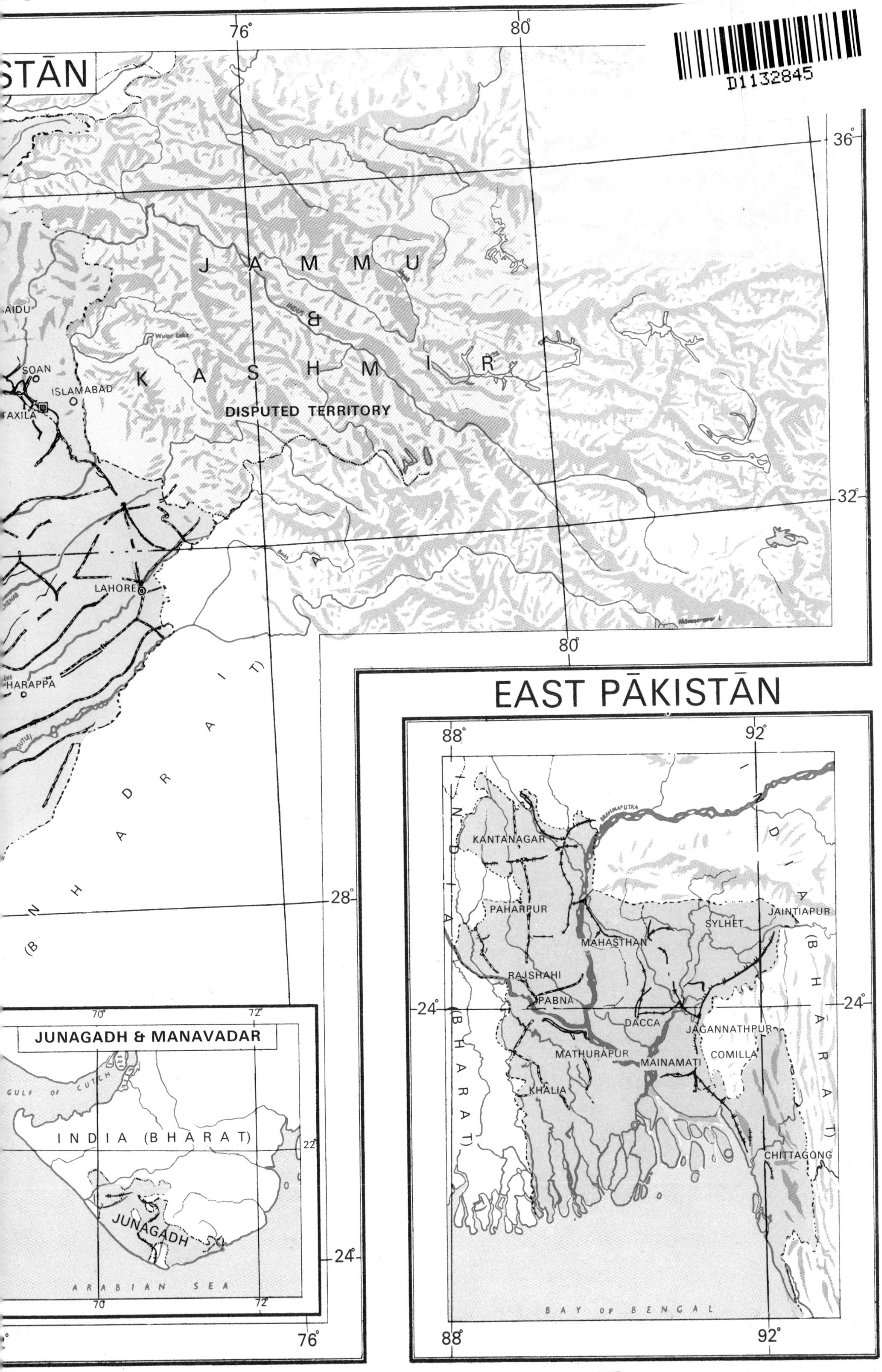

76° 80° 36°

J A M M U

&

K A S H M I R

DISPUTED TERRITORY

32°

AIDU

SOAN
ISLAMABAD
TAXILA

Wular Lake

LAHORE

HARAPPA

80°

EAST PĀKISTĀN

88° 92°

BRAHMAPUTRA

KANTANAGAR

PAHARPUR

SYLHET JAINTIAPUR

MAHASTHAN

RAJSHAHI

28°

PABNA

24° 24°

DACCA JAGANNATHPUR

MATHURAPUR COMILLA

MAINAMATI

KHALIA

CHITTAGONG

(B H A R A T)

(B H A R A T)

BAY of BENGAL

88° 92°

70° 72°

JUNAGADH & MANAVADAR

GULF OF CUTCH

I N D I A (B H Ā R A T)

22°

JUNAGADH

24°

ARABIAN SEA

70° 72°

76°

ARCHITECTURE AND ART TREASURES IN PAKISTAN

ARCHITECTURE
AND ART TREASURES
IN PAKISTAN

Prehistoric, Protohistoric, Buddhist and Hindu Periods

Dr. F. A. KHAN, S.I., T.Pk.,

Director of Archaeology and Museums,
Government of Pakistan.

ELITE PUBLISHERS LIMITED
Karachi

ACKNOWLEDGEMENT

It is my pleasant duty to record my gratefulness to Mr. Q. U. Shahab, S.Q.A., C.S.P., Secretary to the Government of Pakistan, Ministry of Education, whose great interest in archaeology has encouraged me to undertake this publication. My sincere thanks are due to Dr. M. A. Ghafur, Mr. S. A. Naqvi, T.I., Dr. Nazimuddin Ahmed, T.I., Mr. Fazal Qadir, T.I., Mr. R. K. Sarma, Mr. Mirza Mahmud Baig, Librarian, Central Archaeological Library and Mr. H. A. Beg, Photographer, Department of Archaeology, for their unfailing help and co-operation. I am grateful to the Surveyor-General of Pakistan for kindly allowing us to reproduce the map. I am also thankful to Prof. A. H. Dani of the University of Peshawar for his kindly going through the text and to the Directors of Lahore Museum and Peshawar Museum and the Curators of Dacca Museum and Rajshahi Museum for the co-operation they have extended to me. My thanks are no less to Mr. A. Mirza Jamil of Elite Publishers Ltd., Karachi, for his valuable help in the production of the book.

Visualised, processed, printed and published by
ELITE PUBLISHERS LIMITED
D-118, S.I.T.E., Karachi, Pakistan

Contents

Foreword

In the story of man and civilization, Pakistan occupies a unique position. It has evidence of the early Stone Age man, his gradual development and struggle for existence, who roamed in the Soan Valley near Rawalpindi in the interglacial ages, some half a million years ago. In about 5000 B.C. pre-historic villagers are seen established in the foothills of Baluchistan as herdsmen and farmers.

The discovery of Kot Diji in the Upper Indus Valley which flourished between 2800 and 2500 B.C. has added a period of 300 years to the history of Pakistan and provided a continuous link with the world-famous Indus Valley Civilization. With its twin capitals at Harappa and Mohenjodaro, the Indus Culture flourished from 2500 — 1500 B.C. Town planning and the underground system of drainage were the outstanding achievements of these people. Recent discovery of Sarai Khola in the vicinity of Taxila has brought to light cultural remains of the late Neolithic period as well as the Kot Dijian culture.

The historic period of Pakistan begins towards the end of the sixth century B.C. when the north-western part of the country known as Gandhara became a part of the Achaemenid Empire. In course of time, Gandhara developed a distinct school of art as a result of a happy blending between local traditions and the Buddhist belief. The innumerable stupas and monasteries scattered both in the East and the West Wings of Pakistan such as at Taxila, Takht-i-Bahi, Swat, Paharpur, Mainamati and Mahasthangarh bear testimony to the greatness of this culture.

These glorious achievements of Pakistan from the early Stone Age down to the advent of the Muslims, deserve a rightful place in our national history. A book on this fascinating subject by a competent authority, was long overdue. It is happy to note that this publication does not only fulfil the demand but also presents a reliable account based on the latest archaeological researches in the pre-Muslim periods of Pakistan in a single volume.

Q. U. Shahab
Secretary to the Government of Pakistan,
Ministry of Education.

Islamabad, June 7, 1968.

General Introduction

THE antiquity of the cultural heritage of Pakistan is as old as humanity itself. It is in this primeval stage of civilization that the grand and grim drama of man's struggle for existence was enacted in the hunting stage of human history. Since then, various peoples with their varied cultural traits came to this land of ours and have left the legacy of a rich cultural wealth in the form of art and architecture which ultimately became the proud heritage of Pakistan. Cultural relics of a country are the best manifestations of a nation's corporate life and Pakistan is exceptionally fortunate in this respect.

Before the advent of Islam, in the beginning of the 8th century A.C., Pakistan had been the meeting place of the Aryans, Achaemenians, Greeks, Shakas, Parthians and the Kushans each with their distinctive cultural outlook. And thus it became a centre of varied cultural diffusions. It is, indeed, in Pakistan that the West met the East. Striking its roots deep into pre-Islamic traditions, the rich cultural possessions of Pakistan can easily be compared with those of the ancient Middle East. The stream of cultural life, which started flowing on the river banks of Soan in the hoary past of about half a million years back, has been kept in motion even down to the present age in spite of occasional obstructions and intermittent lapses.

Diverse influences of geography, geology, religion and socio-political conditions of a country play a most vital role in the formation and development of its architecture and art treasures, and hence account for the development of varied styles throughout the world. Pakistan is no exception to this rule. Its present geographical limits contain as great a variety of climate as of people. The rainless desert lands of Sind, the rugged mountainous regions of the North-West Frontier and Baluchistan and the land of five rivers — the Punjab, are sharply contrasted with the monotonous flat riverain plains of East Pakistan with torrential rains and refreshing endless greenery.

West Pakistan, from time immemorial, became a hunting ground for foreign invaders as a result of which the region became a gigantic melting pot of varied cultures. All these currents and cross-currents of political, social, religious and climatic influences adequately explain the variety of art and architectural styles evolved in West Pakistan in various periods. But East Pakistan was not exposed to foreign influences to such an extent, being situated in the inaccessible eastern corner of the sub-continent. Consequently it could evolve an indigenous culture of its own in comparative isolation.

The rich deposit of soft alluvium, left annually by the receding flood waters of the innumerable rivers of East Pakistan, is the readily available plastic medium for the manufacture of bricks, sculptured plaques and other art objects.

Thus, the chief building material in most of the monuments of East Pakistan is brick. In addition, bamboo and timber are also available in abundance in this region and these have enormously influenced the style of architecture in East Pakistan by imparting to it a characteristic use of curves.

Soan in the Potwar region of Rawalpindi District is no longer a new name to the pre-historians. In the Soan Valley, we have some of the earliest evidences of stone age man, claiming an antiquity of about half a million years. No human skeleton of that distant antiquity has yet been discovered, but the deposits of crude stone implements which fall within the geological sequence of the Pleistocene period, have yielded valuable specimens.

A distinct series of industries carrying common elements developing through time has been found. These common elements include such well-known forms as the plain flake, varieties of core, and faceted flakes. But, continuous through the series and forming in most industries the prominent feature, are pebble tools made either on unbroken or on fractured pebbles, the latter including peculiar of "flat-based" artifacts. These implements are sufficiently homogeneous to justify their grouping in terms of a single industry which is called the Soan Culture. This has been divided into an early phase and a late one, the latter of which persisted into the Third or even the Fourth Interglacial. (Diorama: National Museum, Karachi).

WEST PAKISTAN

Palaeolithic Age

SOAN

PAKISTAN possesses some of the earliest relics of Stone Age man in the sub-continent, particularly in the Soan Valley of the Potwar region near Rawalpindi, claiming a probable antiquity of about 5,00,000 years. No human skeleton of such distant antiquity has yet been discovered there, but the rough, rugged and crude stone implements recovered from the terraces of the Soan carry the saga of human toil and labour to interglacial periods. The Stone Age men fashioned their implements sufficiently homogeneous to justify their grouping in terms of a culture called Soan culture.

The Potwar region in Rawalpindi district is roughly bounded by the Indus in the west, the Jhelum and Poonch rivers in the east, the Pir Panjal foothills in the north and the Salt Range in the south, the town of Rawalpindi constituting the focal point.

The full understanding of these ancient relics involves a highly technical study of their geological setting. They belong to an age when the climate and the landscape differed materially from those of the present day and when, from time to time, the snow-cap of the Himalayas spread downwards under arctic conditions towards the plains and then, in milder phase, retreated once more into the highlands. These arctic periods are known as periods of "glaciation" and the intervening phases of warm or temperate climate are known as "interglacial periods". During the long era which they cover, it is thought by geologists that there were five of these glacial periods or "ice ages" in Northern India, separated by four interglacials.

In the valley of the river Soan, certain of the "terraces", which have been cut by the river in the material deposited by the melting ice-field during interglacial phases have yielded rough stone implements of more than one kind. The most ancient have been recovered from deposits belonging to the beginning of the Second or "Great" Interglacial period. They consist of crude flakes struck from large pebbles of quartzite. Archaeologists have named them *pre-Soan* to distinguish from the better defined implements of later phases.

The Soan culture has been divided into an early

phase and a late phase, and the latter persisted into the Third or even the Fourth Interglacial. The typical tool of Soan has been designated "Chopper". In its most primitive form, it is struck by means of a stone hammer from a rounded pebble without the preparation of the usual little "platform" from which such flaking is commonly effected, and often has a steep cutting-edge worked on one side only. Other choppers are made from thick flakes with a striking platform. In the late Soan period, there was a marked improvement in technique, particularly in the trimming of the "core" or primary lump of stone before the flake was struck from it.

Alongside the flake "chopper" industry of the Soan region, another class of tool of different kind is also found. In this type, the implement is shaped on the core itself, and the difference is an important one. The characteristic core-tool is the so-called "hand-axe", a pear-shaped or oval implement formed by whittling down the rough, original stone by means of a hammer stone, wood or horn until the desired shape and a continuous cutting-edge are achieved. These stone choppers and hand axes have revealed, so to say, a written chapter to the archaeologist, proving that even in so remote a period, man had proved his intellectual superiority over all other beings. The whole long period, however, is still very obscure and needs much further exploration to trace the Palaeolithic industries of Pakistan to establish their relationship with similar cultures outside the country.

SANGHAO

Another stone industry of considerable importance has been located at Sanghao, an insignificant village at the foot of the hill that separates Buner from the district of Mardan in West Pakistan. The village stands at an elevation of about 1700 feet and the cave lies at an elevation of about 2000 feet near the mouth of one of several canyons with narrow deeply alluviated valleys which debouch east of Sanghao and join to form the piedmont plain which slopes south and west of Swat river. Bed rock near the cave consists of phyllite and schist, and minor calcareous sandstone formation. The cave itself lies within a limestone conglomerate. The deposit is at least 50 feet thick, made up of fragments derived from the erosion of the limestone in the ridges above.

The cave of Parkho-darra, where excavations were carried out by the Peshawar University, originated as an overhanging re-entrant resulting from meander undercutting in limestone deposit of the terrace on the south bank of the Khwar (river-bed). The tools found in the cave confirm that the cave was enlarged and extended by rock-fall and weathering.

The cave consists of three main parts: (i) the main cave; (ii) a fallen portion with a big boulder; and (iii) a low cave separated again by a boulder fall.

The main cave is irregularly made up. The ceiling shows a rough curvature, the underside of which is thickly coated with black soot. At one place there is a deep hollow suggesting that the breaking away from the conglomerate took place at different times.

Excavation in the cave revealed five main periods of which the first three periods, from the bottom, belong to a purely stone age while period IV shows late historic materials datable to the Buddhist period from the second century B.C. to the second century A.C. Period V is a natural deposit which obviously filled in after the second century A.C.

The rock floor of the cave showed a very rough surface occupied by limestone nodules with grit and sand deposited by river action. Period I had been a regular habitation indicated by ash and charcoal left over together with animal bones, teeth, fragments of horns and plenty of quartz tools. Besides quartz, are also found schist fragments including points and edged tools. The size of the tools in Period I is comparatively larger than the tools of the later periods. The period ended with the sudden fall of the boulder from the ceiling.

It is on the top of these boulders that the men of Period II settled and continued occupation for a long period. Period II yielded quartz, red-stained tools, schist fragments, animal teeth and fractured bones.

Period III is a continuation of the stone age material seen earlier and shows regular occupation with plenty of material in the deposit. The quartz tools were again red-stained and other objects include animal horns, hammer-stones of granite, bone fragments, animal teeth and tools made of schist.

The next period IV makes a complete break in the material remains. In this period, no regular occupation was observed in the cave, but several pits were found—all full of ash, charcoal, bones and potsherds. It seems that the cave was used for cooking purposes by the occupants. The date of this period is determined by the discovery of one copper coin of Kanishka, a fragment of local black polished ware and rim

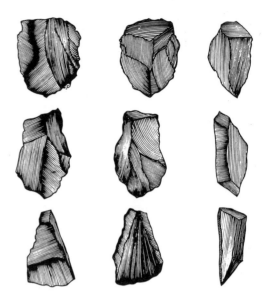

Stone implements, Sanghao Cave, Peshawar University.

fragments of drinking vessels belonging to the Kushana period. The upper-most level of V was a natural deposit.

Stone tools of Sanghao can be divided into three groups namely (1) quartz tools, (2) schist fragments and (3) hammer-stones and anvils. Quartz is the most common raw material that has been used by the Sanghao cave man. The entire tool complex of Sanghao represents a h o m o g e n e o u s technique throughout, the only fundamental difference being that the size of tools in the two later periods is smaller than that in Period I.

A large number of schist and limestone pieces were recovered from Sanghao cave. Some of them were used for lining the pits and others for making rough ovens. A few of them might have been used as a ground base for breaking bones or even hammering the quartz into flaking. About a dozen hammer-stones were found with three pieces of horn. All the stones are river-rolled pebbles of granite—a variety of stone found in the Malakand ridge and must have been quarried from the river-bed. They are of different shapes of which rounded and flat varieties are prominent.

The Sanghao stone industry is predominantly a flake industry. The nearest comparable material comes from the Potwar region where similar flake tools were collected in large quantity. It is from that very source that the Indian Middle Stone Age has to be derived through the intermediary of Pakistan. It is just possible that future excavation at Sanghao may bring forth the anthropological evidence of the particular race of man responsible for the spread of this culture in this part of the world.

Late Neolithic and Bronze Age

RURAL COMMUNITIES OF BALUCHISTAN

SOME 6,000 years ago, there grew up amidst the rugged wind-swept valleys and foot-hills of Baluchistan, small village communities taking the first hesitant steps in human progress. Here, we find a more continuous story of human activity—though still in the Stone Age. We find these prehistoric villagers already established both as herdsmen and as farmers. They are found settled in villages, in the valleys of the hills or on the out-skirts of the plains with cattle, sheep and goats, growing barley and other crops. This early struggle on the threshold of civilization is, indeed, a fascinating study. But there is at present a long and unbridged gap between these early agriculturists and their Stone Age predecessors which awaits filling up, in order to reconstruct the actual position of Pakistan in this vital phase of growth and experiment which ultimately culminated in the great civilizations of ancient Mesopotamia on the one side and the Indus Valley on the other.

Painted pot, Nindowari, French Archaeological Mission in Pakistan

Painted pot, Ispelinji, Department of Archaeology, Pakistan

The village cultures of Baluchistan are the by-product of folk-movements from the Iranian plateau in that remote time due possibly to some geographical or political reasons. These cultures are generally discovered on and in artificial mounds which are, in fact, the results of successive rebuilding of small settlements on the remains of its predecessors, so that age by age the mound rose upon its own dead self. The free use of mud or mud-bricks for walling contributed to this process. Careful excavations of these mounds and the classification of their contents, layer by layer, have grouped them into two main categories of culture based on pottery technique and geographical distribution. The first group, popularly known as Zhob culture, is centred in North Baluchistan while the second comprises the Quetta, Amri, Nal and Kulli cultures of Sind and South Baluchistan.

The best known site of Zhob valley is that of Rana Ghundai, situated about 8 miles east of Loralai, in North Baluchistan. The earliest occupants of the site were apparently nomadic herdsmen who left hearths but no houses. Their pottery was made without the potter's wheel and was almost entirely unpainted. After a considerable lapse of time, they were succeeded by a people who built houses with boulder-footings and produced excellent specimens of wheel-made pottery ranging in colour from buff to a dark terracotta. On this they painted black friezes of fine stylized humped bulls and black bucks together with geometric patterns. The typical pot-shape of the period is a narrow footed bowl. Both shape and decoration are comparable with those of early pottery from the sites of north-eastern Iran and this second Rana Ghundai culture can be dated to a time much before 3000 B.C. This culture was again followed by a third and more enduring culture the potters of which added red to their colour scheme and used it on the normal red background. A characteristic pot-form was a small goblet on a pedestal-foot.

Burnished pot, Sarai Khola, Department of Archaeology, Pakistan

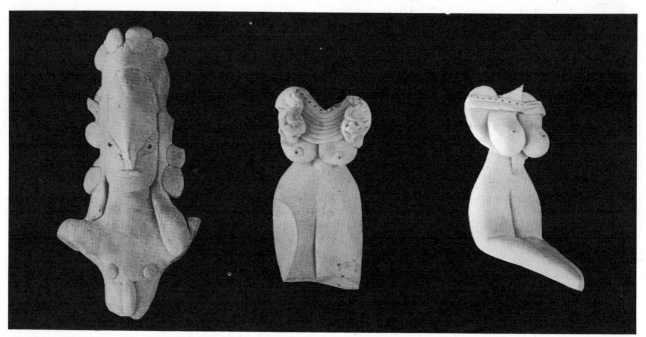

Terracotta figurines, Zhob Valley, Department of Archaeology, Pakistan

This third phase is represented by three successive building levels thus indicating long duration. It was succeeded by a new settlement associated with a completely different equipment including large bowls of coarse ware with applied strip or cordons and with floral designs painted in brown, black or purplish-red. Thereafter though occupation continued, all painted pottery ceased. The terracotta figurines recovered in the course of excavations appear to belong to the third phase of Rana Ghundai and can be ascribed to the third millennium B.C. These terracotta objects include humped bulls and female figures narrow at the waist, mounted on small pedestals and adorned with necklaces.

Of the cultures of Sind and South Baluchistan, the Quetta culture was found to be extending southwards to Kalat. The pottery is painted in a geometric style in purplish-brown or black paint on a buff ground. The designs include chevrons formed by combining thick and thin bands, diagonally divided squares, pairs of opposed triangles, distinctive stepped and oval motifs. This ware, buff in colour, is comparable with the early pottery at Tal-i-Bakun and Susa in southern Iran and may be dated before 3000 B.C.

It is difficult to find Iranian parallels in the Amri culture of Sind and the Nal culture of Baluchistan. Whatever may be their origin, it is certain that they developed for a long time in the regions where we

INCHES

CMS

Drinking pots, Zhob Valley, Department of Archaeology, Pakistan

find them. They possess certain common features. The terracotta figurines which are the characteristic of other groups are absent. Their pottery is generally of thin and fine texture and has a buff or pinkish paste covered with a white slip as a basis for painted ornament. This is outlined in black and brownish paint having red as secondary colour and occasionally yellow, blue and green. The designs include panels framed in multiple lines and sometimes filled with black and white chequers, and bands of diamond, chevron, loop and scale-pattern. Animal designs occur both at Nal and Amri. Chert blades are very frequent in both the sites while Nal yielded two hoards of copper implements which include flat axes of primitive type, an elongated chisel, a tanged knife and a straight-sided saw. These are comparable

General view of site, Sarai Khola

Great Granary, Harappa

17

Excavated graves, Sarai Khola

with types from the Indus Civilization.

The villages in which the Amri-Nal people lived were occasionally defended by stone walls and bastions, their houses having stone foundation courses. At Nal, an extensive cemetery of this culture has yielded about 100 graves. An important feature of Amri culture is that at Amri and certain other sites it has been found below the very distinctive Indus Valley culture. There is, however, no evidence to prove that the Amri-Nal culture contributed directly to the formation of the Indus Civilization. It represents merely one of the local developments which constituted the environment for the growth of the Indus Civilization.

The Kulli culture of South Baluchistan include the mounds of Mehi and Shahi-Tump. It is characterized by a number of clay figurines of women and animals, clay birds and clay model carts and in this and some other respects it tends to be more close to the Indus Culture. The pottery is usually buff, with whitish or pinkish slip, having painted ornamentation in black or sometimes with horizontal bands in red. The usual pottery forms are globular beakers, tall bottle-shaped vases, small flat dishes and straight sided cups and jars. The distinctive painted decoration consists of a frieze of conventional animals and plants. The background is often filled with birds and beetles and also with rosettes and other symbols. Occasional occurrence of black-on-red pottery, tall dishes on-stands and the pipal leaf etc., in pottery decoration indicates affinity at some stage with the Indus Culture. Other objects illustrating this culture include copper pins, agate and lapis lazuli beads, copper mirrors, copper and clay bracelets, saddlequerns and chert blades.

The Kulli culture people are known to have lived in houses with walls built either of rubble set in mud mortar or of squared stone blocks. The walls were occasionally faced with white paste, the average size

18

Covered Drains, Harappa

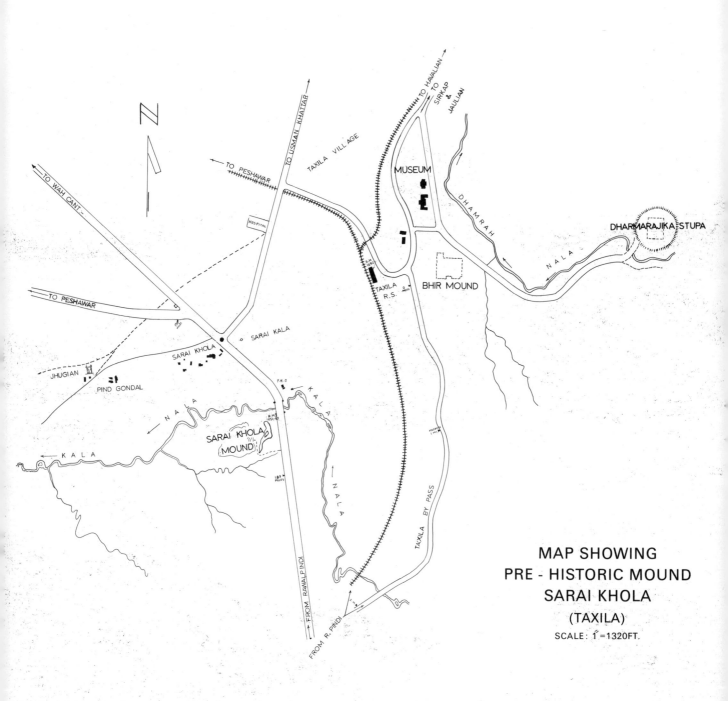

MAP SHOWING
PRE - HISTORIC MOUND
SARAI KHOLA
(TAXILA)
SCALE : 1" =1320FT.

Excavated remains, Harappa

of the rooms being 12 ft x 8 ft. At Mehi, there was evidence of cremation-burial both in pots and without. Of the clay female figurines, which end at the waist in pedestal, the hands are represented resting on hips, the face is squeezed out into a birdlike form with applied pellets for eyes, and the hair style is elaborate. The date of Kulli culture can be ascribed to sometime in the first half of the third millennium B.C.

SARAI KHOLA

Before the discovery of Sarai Khola, a pre-historic settlement of great importance in the vicinity of Taxila, it was believed that the Gandhara region was without any pre-historic settlement. But the discovery of Sarai Khola has necessitated a change of view and the history of Taxila has been pushed back by nearly 2,400 years from 600 B.C. to 3000 B.C. The discovery of Sarai Khola has thus opened a new and highly interesting chapter in the history of Pakistan.

Situated amidst beautiful and picturesque surroundings, Sarai Khola stands prominent on the southern bank of the Kala Nala, on the Grand Trunk Road at a distance of about two miles south-west of the Bhir Mound, the earliest of the settlements at Taxila. The mound which rises in four successive terraces measures about 2,000 feet north-south and 1,000 feet east-west. The depth of the cultural deposits is more than 14 feet.

Stone implements, Sarai Khola, Department of Archaeology, Pakistan

The surface collection from Sarai Khola comprise stone celts, chert blades, cores, a stone arrow head, scrapers, terracotta animal and female figurines, clay bangles, stone and paste beads, copper pins and a wide range of hand-made and wheel turned pottery, burnished, plain and painted.

The Sarai Khola wheel-made pottery is of medium texture. The rims are short beaded or slightly averted. The main forms of pottery include band around the neck in red sepia or black straight horizontal lines, wavy loops and hatched designs. This pottery in form, decoration and colour scheme is almost identical with that of the pre-Harappan sites of Kot Diji. Jalilpur, Bhoot and the pre-citadel levels of Harappa.

Excavations at Sarai Khola have brought to light three cultural sequences, namely, historic at the top, Kot Dijian in the middle and late Neolithic at the bottom. Important among the late period materials, is a terracotta bejewelled female figurine and also terracotta bulls with well marked features. The Kot Dijian period is represented by a large collection of pottery with medium body, short beaded or slightly averted rims, fugitive band around the neck in red, brown, sepia or warm black painted on dull red slip.

Section showing various occupation levels, Sarai Khola

22

Workers' platforms, Harappa

23

Other finds include flint blades, terracotta and shell bangle fragments. The late Neolithic period yielded a stone celt and a thin flint blade and highly burnished brown pottery made on slow wheel.

Excavations at Sarai Khola also brought to light about fifty graves of outstanding character where the skeletal remains were found to be lying from east to west with faces turned towards either north or south. These graves are of two periods. One very noticeable feature of these graves was the absence of funeral goods. Parallel to these cemeteries are not available anywhere in the sub-continent. The Sarai Khola finds

Harappan date immediately below the Indus levels, with the help of which it has been possible to push back the pre-history of Pakistan for another 300 years i.e., from 2500 B.C. to 2800 B.C.

The people of Kot Diji were in possession of a developed and sophisticated culture with a superior skill in pot-making which, as it appears, greatly influenced the Indus people of later date in certain ceramic motifs, town-planning and fortification as well.

The site of Kot Diji consists of two parts: the high citadel mound and the outside lower city. The citadel

General view of excavations, Kot Diji

have thus started to open a new chapter in the ancient history of Pakistan which so long remained shrouded in myth.

KOT DIJI

The pre-historic site of Kot Diji in the Khairpur Division of West Pakistan has furnished information of high significance in relation to the Indus Civilization. Evidence of the early stage of the Indus Civilization in some forms were unearthed at this site, but the most important aspect of Kot Diji excavation is the existence of a new cultural element of pre-

area again represents two definite cultural phases— the mature Indus culture in the upper levels and a hitherto unknown new culture of the Kot Dijians in the lower levels, both separated from each other by a thick accumulation of charred material. The Kot Diji culture is distinguished by a completely new type of ceramic technique.

The upper Indus levels of Kot Diji represented extensive, well-planned building remains, with stone foundations and mud brick super-structures, separated by lanes and streets. Cultural material includes

24

black-on-red pottery with familiar motifs of pipal leaf, intersecting circles, peacock, antelope, sun and various geometric and incised decorations.

The intermediate, thick burnt deposit shows a sudden break in the cultural sequence of the site and suggests the burning of the earlier settlement of the Kot Dijians by the later Harappans.

The Kot Dijian occupation levels are marked by massive walls of mud brick on stone foundations. The most interesting feature of this level is its massive defence wall around the citadel area—one of the earliest known fortification walls in the sub-continent.

features are a fine thin body, short beaded or slightly averted rim and a broad band round the neck in red, brown, sepia or warm black, painted on a cream or dull red slip. The pottery is wheel made and its ground varies from pinkish to red. The broad features of this pottery remained unchanged however throughout the Kot Dijian occupation, yet some stages of new development in decoration, texture and form were also noticed. The thin textured squat globular form and almost rimless and neckless open mouthed features of earlier stage pottery developed in later stages with more pronounced neck and rim.

Its solidity and massiveness suggest that it was the creation of a highly organized community. It was raised on bed-rock with undressed stone blocks at the base to support a mud-brick superstructure. The wall was again strengthened externally with bastions at irregular intervals. It sometimes served as a back wall for the residential quarters close to the defence wall inside the citadel. During the subsequent Harappan occupation, it fell into disuse.

The pottery finds of Kot Diji levels constitute the principal element of this new culture. Its distinctive

In the earlier stages, decoration was confined exclusively to a characteristic neck-band which, in a later period, was replaced by the horizontal and wavy lines, single loops, roundels and simple triangular patterns.

Other forms in pottery include dish-on-stand, both squat and long type, thin and delicate vases, flat-based and straight-walled cylindrical vases, bowls, shallow plates of thin grey fabric, beakers, jar-covers and lids. This thin and light ware stands in sharp contrast to the Harappan thick and heavy pottery. The rimless Kot Dijian pottery has affinity with the pottery re-

Drains, Mohenjodaro

covered from under the mud brick defences at Harappa and also to some extent with that from the lower levels at Amri. These parallels indicate that this culture was not an isolated and unrelated one.

Minor objects in terracotta, stone, shell, bone and metal representing the Indus culture are abundant in the upper Harappan levels, but a sharp decrease in their frequency is noticed in the lower levels representing the Kot Dijian culture. Of all the minor antiquities from Kot Diji levels long, sharp and thin blades and fine micro-blades in stone, toys, plain and painted bangles, cakes, cone and beads and also a beautifully modelled bull figurine in terracotta, deserve special mention.

AMRI

Amri, in the district of Dadu, is a small village on the right bank of the Indus. The ancient site was found strewn with innumerable potsherds of great antiquarian value. From a comparative examination of pottery and other miscellaneous objects, the occupation at Amri appears to be of longer duration. The successive layers and corresponding levels can be divided into five periods of which the first four are pre-historic while the last is the period of Muslim occupation. The pre-historic phases of Amri can be

dated from the beginning of the 3rd millenium B.C. to the middle of the 1st millenium B.C. without any noticeable break in the chronological sequences. The Muslim occupation of the site began in the 16th century A.C.

The Amri culture is mainly represented by its classic pottery. Period I shows some evolution in the technique of pottery making and its decoration. Pottery of the lowest period is all hand-made having decoration in black and red. Decoration is mostly geometrical and of rough type. Most of the pots and vases are rimless, thin-walled and carefully decorated. No structural remains could be found in this level.

With the rising of the occupation level, a new type of decoration on a leather coloured background of triangles opposed by their bases and disposed on either sides of a double band is met with. This design is thick and heavy and the triangles have red filling. Between them, are various patterns of broken or wavy lines in groups, ladders and so on. For the first time, a type of dish-on-stand is found. In addition, a few bone tools and a large number of chert blades were also recovered from this level.

Later in Period I, phase II was found in its maximum extension on the site. Flat rectangular houses with doors and mud floorings containing interred jars were exposed at this level. Chert blades, flakes and cores were found in abundance. The pottery of this level is wheel-made and is mostly decorated with a net-motif having triangular black half-fillings. During this phase, the potters' art marked a definite improvement both in technique and decoration.

The last phase of Period I is the immediate continuation of the earlier one, but of shorter duration. It is manifested by one structural level only. During this phase, the same process of improvement in ceramics went on. The colour was now used not only in bands, but also as a filling for the design and animals are frequently represented in the decoration. In spite of changes and evolution, the entire phase of Period I demonstrates a unity and continuity.

Period II of Amri did not make any notable break with the earlier one. In this period two phases were noticed. In the first phase, the Harappan type of pottery appeared increasingly and, at the same time, many shapes and designs of the early Amri phases were still in use. The second phase of Period II was marked by an enlarged platform made of mud bricks with post-holes on it. This phase showed Harappan pottery in increasing numbers. The typical Amri pottery was also in use.

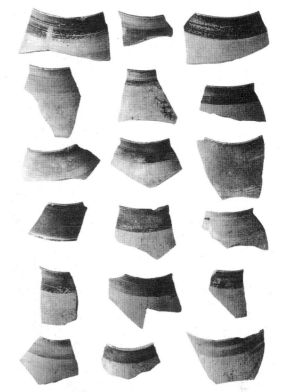

Painted pottery, Kot Diji, Department of Archaeology, Pakistan.

Painted pottery, Sarai Khola, Department of Archaeology, Pakistan

Painted pot, Amri, Mohenjodaro Museum

objects of Mohenjodaro and Harappa. Period III of Amri also showed four phases. The first phase was marked by pottery finds of black-on-red. Shapes and motifs are also identical with those found in the Indus cities. Judged by the material collected, the second phase stands very close to phase I. Pottery of this phase II is almost identical with that of phase I. Some new types, such as, a basin with averted rim and a high pedestalled dish-on-stand with a swelling upper part of the shaft, were introduced.

In the third phase, burnt bricks were noticed for the first time and their size was the same as noted at Harappa and Mohenjodaro. Phase III of Period III yielded the same specimens of pottery but they showed not only innovation in shapes but almost a revolution in decoration. Instead of the usual Harappan black-on-red, we see either a polished chocolate or brown-reddish slip or dull pinkish-violet. As for decoration, it is usually applied with a heavy brush. A steatite Harappan seal, without inscription, bearing a three-headed animal and three cubic marble weights in the Harappan norms were also found in this phase. A great abundance of pottery and a fragmentary stone seal of Indus culture were the only finds from the fourth phase of Period III.

The fourth period of Amri showed, for the first time, some specimens of Jhangar type. They include grey ware with external polish and incised decoration.

From the start, Amri culture appears to be a blend of local elements similar to those of Kot Diji, with Baluchi adjuncts. Except for a temporary break in Period III, contacts with Baluchistan are a constant trait at Amri.

INDUS VALLEY CIVILIZATION

When the primitive village communities in the

Period III of Amri can broadly be called the Indus Valley culture because almost all the finds of this period have a clear affinity with the Indus Valley

Burial pottery, Harappa Museum

*Jar painted with fish-scale pattern, Kot Diji,
National Museum, Karachi*

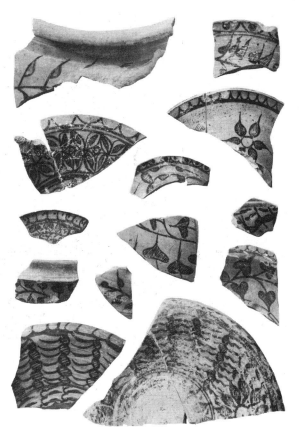

*Painted pottery, Kot Diji, Department of
Archaeology, Pakistan*

Water pitcher painted with a horned deity, Kot Diji, National Museum, Karachi

Burial pot, Harappa, National Museum, Karachi

sion that the latter was, in part, contemporary with the Early Dynastic Sumerian Culture.

The fertile valley of the hydrographic system of the Indus and the easy means of communications and transportation, which these rivers afforded, were the basis of the economy of the Indus people. With these advantages, they had early trade-links with the contemporary neighbouring cities of Iran and Mesopotamia. These agrarian people cultivated wheat, sesame, dates and cotton and for the irrigation of the fields the farmers depended on annual rainfall and floods. The existence of brick-lined street drains and rain water pipes, the universal use of burnt bricks in construction work and the representation on seals of such moist habitating animals as the tiger, the rhinoceros, the elephant and the buffalo prove that the Indus Valley enjoyed a heavier rainfall in ancient times. The surplus agricultural production was bartered in kind against such articles as metals, semi-precious stones and other miscellaneous commodities imported from the neighbouring countries.

Baluchistan area were still struggling against a difficult highland environment and when a very highly cultured people were trying to assert themselves at Kot Diji, there flourished, between the years 2500 and 1500 B.C., one of the most well-developed urban civilizations of the ancient world namely in the Indus Valley cities of Mohenjodaro and Harappa. The Indus Valley people possessed a high standard of art and craftsmanship and a well developed system of pictographic writing.

One of the chief characteristic features of this civilization is the conspicuous absence of iron and the frequent use of copper and bronze objects side by side with stone implements. The close resemblance between some of the antiquities of southern Mesopotamia and the Indus Valley has led to the conclu-

The Indus Valley architecture is plain and utilitarian. Neither imposing temples, as in Sumer, nor royal tombs, as at Ur and in Egypt, are found here. The aim of the city builders, as it seems, was to make life comfortable rather than luxurious. The houses which were well planned provided comfortable living. The drains of the Indus Valley cities are among their chief achievements. The system is certainly the most elaborate ancient system as yet discovered and can easily be termed modern in character.

The most remarkable building at Harappa is the "Great Granary" and no less striking is the "Great Bath" at Mohenjodaro. The Granary may well have served the purpose of a public treasury. The Great Bath of Mohenjodaro may have been used for religious or ceremonial bathings, as many of the common

Pottery, Harappa Museum   *Pottery, Harappa Museum*

MOHENJODARO
PLAN OF HOUSES AND STREETS

HR. AREA
A&B SECTIONS
Scale in feet

31

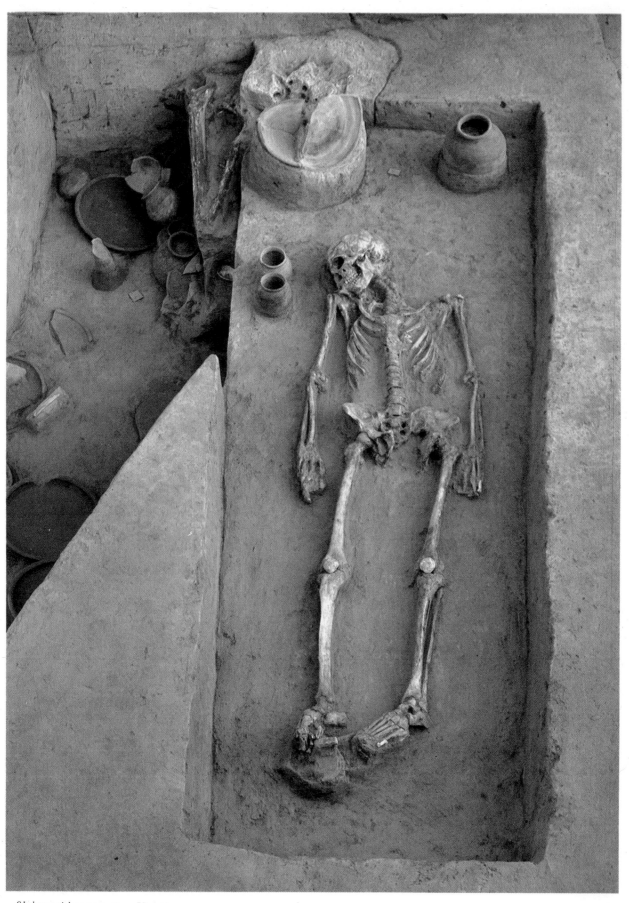

Skeleton with grave pottery, Harappa

dwellings both at Harappa and Mohenjodaro possessed their own bathrooms and wells.

These ancient cities have yielded various art objects of which a large number of burnt clay, male and female figurines and models of animals and birds are prominent. Bedecked with profuse jewellery and pannier-like arrangements on each side of their head, the female figurines wear short skirts round their loins. Some of the panniers are stained by smoke, possibly due to the burning of oil or incense in them. These figurines perhaps represent the "Mother Goddess" whose cult was also popular in the Near Middle East in ancient times. The few male figurines are mostly nude, but bearded and wear long hair at the back. They were all modelled by hand and painted light red.

The steatite bust of a king-priest or a nobleman in the round, wearing a loose robe with an engraved trefoil pattern in relief is a unique specimen of sculptural art from Mohenjodaro.

The figural art is best illustrated by steatite seals with life-like representations of animals such as the Brahmani bull, the short-horned bull, the buffalo, tiger, rhinoceros, crocodile and also mythological figures like the Unicorn. There are also human figures with horns and tail, and a horned tiger. The seals also bear short pictographic inscriptions which, however, still await decipherment. But some of the scenes depicted on seals give a clue to the religious belief of the people.

An excellent example of plastic art is displayed in the small dancing girl in bronze from Mohenjodaro. With a realistically portrayed rhythmic swing of the body and with an effective modelling of hips and back, the dancing girl from Mohenjodaro shows a slim figure with flat negroid features.

Among the ornaments, the most common are necklaces and pendants of beads of semi-precious stones. Ornaments of faience and paste beads are also fairly popular while those of shell and clay are less frequent. Square, disc-shaped, etched cornelian beads decorated with white designs are also found. Beads of similar technique also come from Mesopotamia and Iran. These strongly suggest a trade in ancient times between the Indus Valley and her western neighbours. Gold necklaces, fillets for head-wear, armlets, bangles and finger rings were worn by both men and women, while long cornelian beads, ear-rings and anklets were exclusively for women.

The chert stone implements are mostly long flakes, evidently for cutting meat and vegetables. Stone vessels are comparatively rare and are more frequently made of alabaster. Most of these vessels are thick and clumsy. A large number of highly polished stone weights are made of chert, quartzite, alabaster, lime-stone and jasper. They are mostly cubical.

The Indus Valley people used copper and bronze for making utensils, implements, statuettes and ornaments. The utensils consist of cooking pots, flat dishes, vases and dishes with covers. The pottery, both plain and painted, occurs in abundance. It is artistic and sophisticated in style which is, again, best demonstrated by the pleasing decoration on the red ware. The designs consist of geometric devices, as well as stylized human, animal and bird forms and also vegetation. Of the geometric patterns, the most elaborate and characteristic design is the intersecting circle. Other decorative elements include the 'fish-scale' pattern and pipal leaf motif. The chess-board design also occurs. Embossed and stamped pottery is fairly common. The Indus Valley pottery in general show a highly developed technique which is evident from the varied shapes.

Whatever may be the origin of the authors of the Indus Valley culture, it is certain that they were highly civilized and of non-Aryan racial stock. These points are attested by the discoveries of their well-built cities and the various aspects of their religion which included the cult of "Mother Goddess", and, trees and animal worship.

The skeletal remains unearthed from the Harappa cemetery include four racial types—the Proto-Australoid, Mediterranean, Alpine and Mongoloid. The Indus Valley people consisted in the main the second type.

Excavations at Harappa, to the south of the citadel mound brought to light a regular cemetery known as R 37 of Harappa period. The bodies were extended from north to south and the burials contained large number from fifteen to forty. The dead wore ornaments, shell bangles, necklaces, anklets of paste beads, copper finger rings and ear-rings of thin copper wire. Toilet articles included handled copper-mirrors, antimony rods, shell spoons and mother of pearl shells. One of the burials contained a pottery lamp and the bones of a fowl.

Two of the burials showed interesting features. One of them was internally lined with mud-bricks. In the other burial, the body had been buried in a wooden coffin. A copper ring was found in the middle finger of the right hand of the body and a shell ring lay to the left shoulder. The burial contained thirty seven pottery vessels: only one was inside the coffin while the remaining lay near and against its head.

To the south of the citadel mound, a post-Harappan period cemetery, termed cemetery 'H', was brought to light. The burials of this cemetery are too meagre to be considered typical of the main body of the population, and must, therefore, be regarded as pertaining to a small section. The cemetery 'H' burials

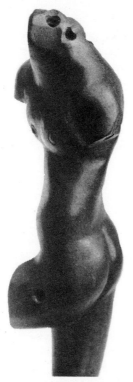

Replica of a dancing torso, original in limestone, Harappa Museum

Replica of a torso, original in limestone, Harappa Museum

cemetery 'H', constitute a system of fractional burials. Only babies were found complete in the embryonic position. The jar mouths were closed by lids or by pots.

The large number of jar burials found in the upper stratum are apparently of a later date and from the fact that the skulls and bones were found in them show no sign of being burnt. It has, therefore, been suggested that the bodies were exposed to the birds and the bones collected later for inhumation. If this view is correct, then we have here a link with the burial custom of the Zoroastrians, but other circum-

fall in two categories referable to an earlier and later strata of occupation. The lower stratum of burials show examples of complete inhumation in which the body was laid generally with hands turned up, the knees bent and the head towards east or north-east, surrounded by pottery, jars, cups, dishes and bowls.

By far the largest number of burials containing skulls and bones found in the upper stratum of

Terracotta toycock, Harappa, National Museum, Karachi

stances do not confirm the supposition that a cognate people was inhabiting the Indus cities.

The pottery associated with the funeral remains, unearthed from cemetery 'H', is of a distinct type which could not be compared with the pottery in use in the Harappan culture cities. The decorations of vegetable patterns and animal representations are peculiar and the forms of vessels are also unlike those represented in the pottery of Harappa and Mohenjo-daro. Certain animal designs depict composite representations: deer with long horns and antlers and also peacocks. The presence of peacocks on these

General view of citadel area with the Kushan period stupa in the background, Mohenjodaro

The Great Bath, Mohenjodaro

Excavated remains of the citadel area, Mohenjodaro

Excavated remains, Mohenjodaro

Excavated remains, Mohenjodaro

General view of Stupa, Mohenjodaro

Main street, Mohenjodaro

A low lane, Mohenjodaro

43

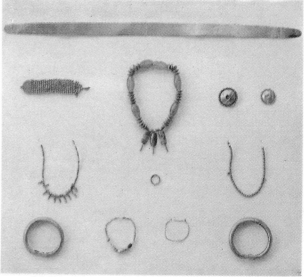

Jewellery, Mohenjodaro Museum

Jewellery, Harappa, National Museum, Karachi

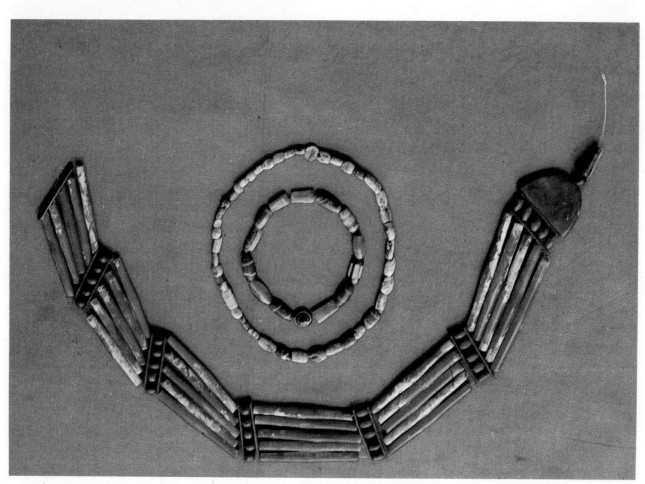

Bead necklaces, Mohenjodaro, National Museum, Karachi

44

Terracotta figurine of mother goddess, Mohenjodaro, National Museum, Karachi

A well inside a house, Mohenjodaro

Building remains, Mohenjodaro

Excavated remains, Mohenjodaro

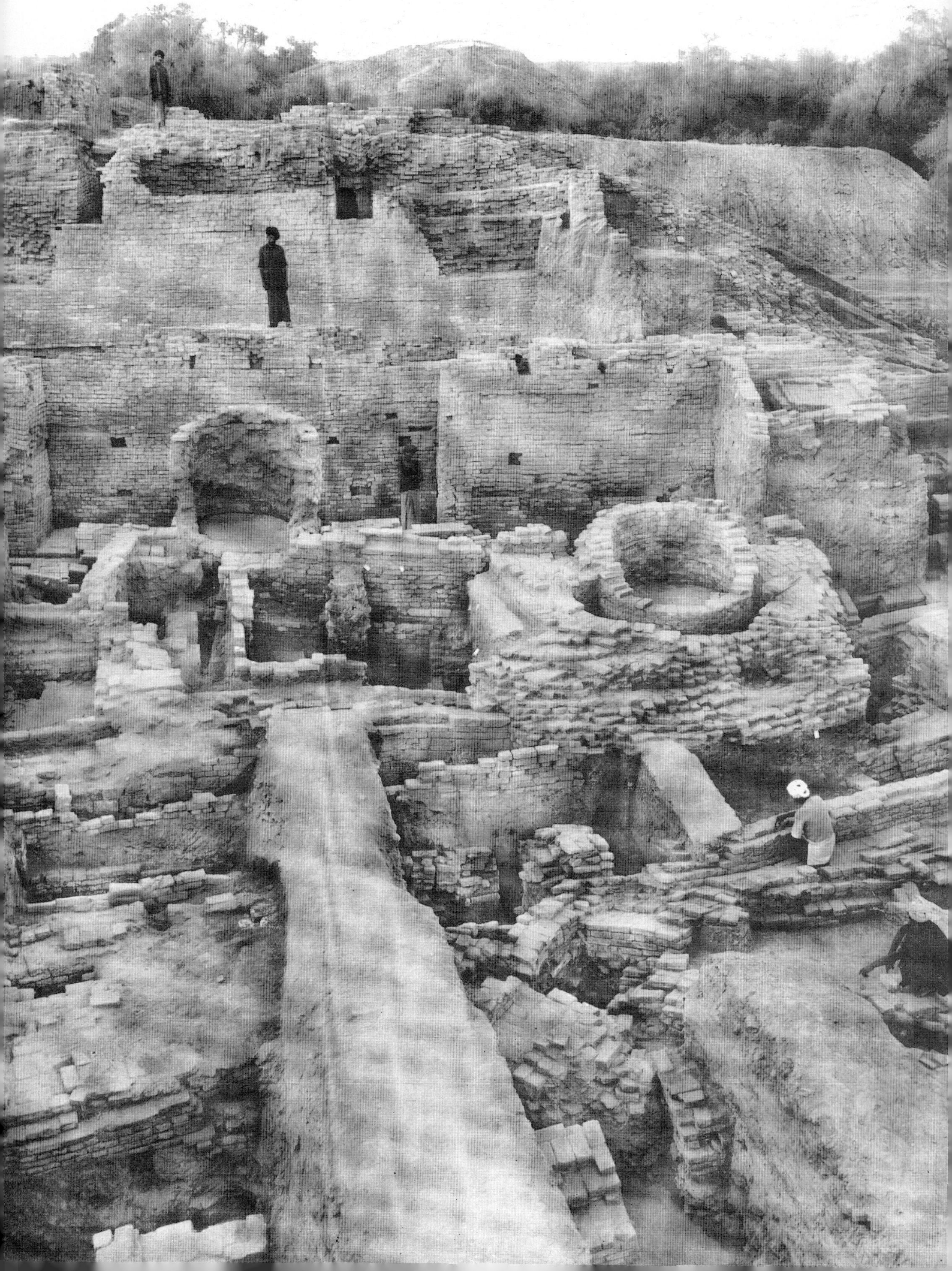

King Priest, Mohenjodaro
National Museum, Karachi

Terracotta figurines of mother goddess, Harappa, National Museum, Karachi

funerary vessels indicates that they were in some way connected with the ideas of after-life.

Among the causes for the decay and desertion of the ancient cities of the Indus Valley after 1800 B.C. progressive climatic changes may have been one. Both the cities being situated on river banks, the growing danger of floods may be another cause for the evacuation of these cities. Moreover, a gradual decline in the material prosperity of the people may have been a contributory cause for the decline of this civilization. There is a dearth of weapons and it is probable that these rich cities with an un-warlike mercantile populace were either ransacked by invading tribes from the hilly regions of Baluchistan or that the inhabitants were compelled to migrate to more fertile valleys when a dry and arid climate began to prevail in the Indus Valley.

The proto-historic site of Chanhudaro, some eighty miles south-west of Mohenjodaro, can mainly be called a post-Harappan site. It is at Chanhudaro that evidence of invasion by foreign invaders comes to light. This settlement shows three distinct cultural sequences; Harappan at the bottom, Jhukar in the middle and Jhangar on top.

The Harappans, whose cultural material is well-

Terracotta head of mother goddess, Harappa, National Museum, Karachi

marked, deserted this settlement after a long period of occupation. They were succeeded by a poorer folk, known as the representatives of the Jhukar culture, who re-used some of the derelict houses and supplemented them with rectangular hovels of matting, paved with broken brick.

The material culture, represented among these primitive habitations includes pottery, stamp-seals, amulets, beads, metal tools and pins, bone awls and a pottery head-rest. The Jhukar pottery seems to combine a variety of elements in which Baluchi and probably Harappa motifs predominate with an underlying Amri strain. On the whole, there seems no reason to regard Jhukar pottery as anything but a native product arising out of the disturbed conditions and folk-movements after the fall of the Indus Valley culture.

The Jhukar pottery is buff with a varied repertoire of decoration painted in black and red. The forms include small footed jars, bottles, offering-stands and saucers with a loop on the edge. The range of decoration is quite varied and employs geometric and stylized plant forms, broad horizontal bands in red, close set chevrons in black and bright red, multiple loops, 'ball-and-stem' motifs and also occasional animal representations. The Jhukar uninscribed circular seals and seal-amulets of pottery or faience, bearing crude decoration, lack all the delicate realism of the Indus series. The beads also point in the same direction.

Burial Jar, Harappa, National Museum, Karachi

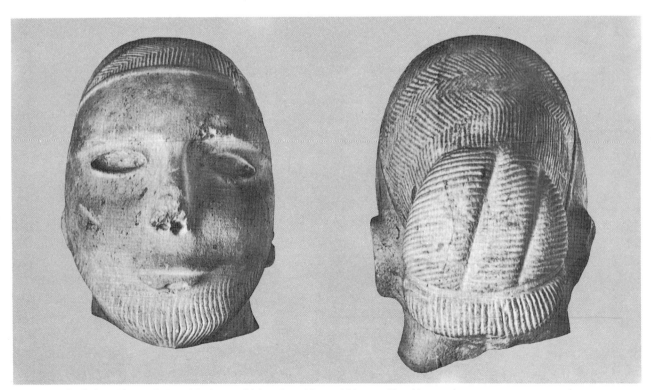

Steatite head of an old man, front and back view, Mohenjodaro, National Museum, Karachi

The West street, Mohenjodaro

The numerous bone awls used for mat-weaving stress the primitive character of the Jhukar culture. The gaily decorated pottery head-rest is a pleasant find from Chanhudaro.

The evidence of Jhukar material particularly the pottery appears to represent a more or less indigenous type in a later stage of evolution, but other portable objects, such as seals, beads, metal implements and weapons, and the use of hair pins suggest the arrival of a new people in the region who were the destroyers of the Indus Civilization.

The final phase of the Chanhudaro occupation is termed the Jhangar culture which appears after the Jhukar settlement. Little is known of this culture except that it marks a break with the old painted pottery traditions. Jhangar culture is characterized by plain incised grey pottery with a primitive appearance. This may represent a purely local culture restricted to a small tribe.

Terracotta figurine of mother goddess profusely adorned with jewellery, Mohenjodaro, National Museum, Karachi

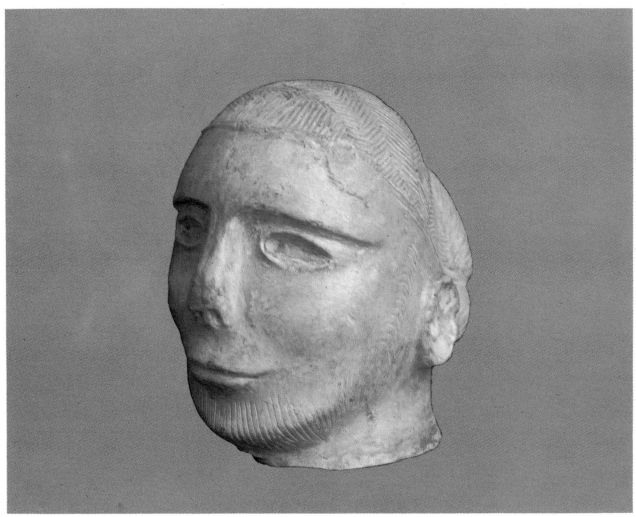

Head of an old man, Mohenjodaro, National Museum, Karachi

Workmen quarters, Harappa

Replica of the dancing girl in bronze, Mohenjodaro, National Museum, Karachi

Terracotta female figurine, Mohenjodaro,
National Museum, Karachi

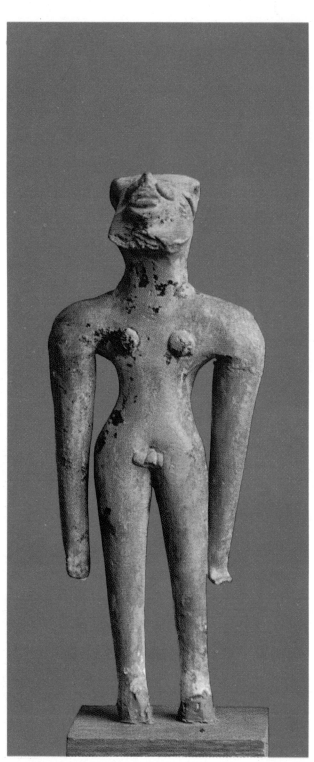

Terracotta male figurine, Mohenjodaro,
National Museum, Karachi

Seal showing the Unicorn, Mohenjodaro,
National Museum, Karachi

Steatite seal of a Unicorn, Mohenjodaro,
National Museum, Karachi

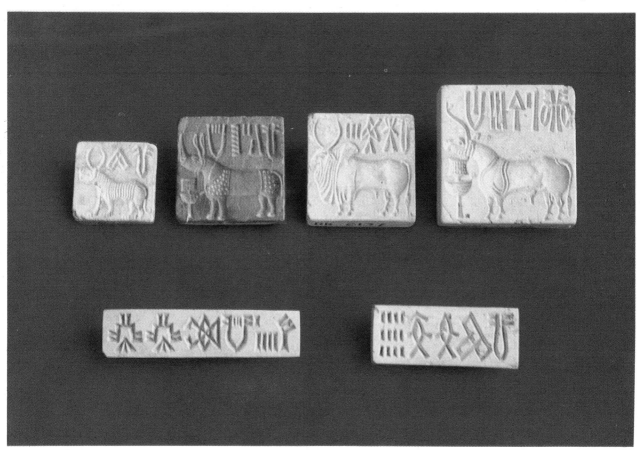

Steatite seals, Mohenjodaro, National Museum, Karachi

Terracotta toy figurines, Mohenjodaro, National Museum, Karachi

Terracotta toy chariot, Mohenjodaro, National Museum, Karachi

Painted pottery, Mohenjodaro, National Museum, Karachi

Burial pottery, Harappa Museum

Copper utensils, Mohenjodaro, National Museum, Karachi

59

Plain pottery, Mohenjodaro, National Museum, Karachi

Plain pottery vases, Mohenjodaro, National Museum, Karachi

Stone weights, Mohenjodaro, National Museum, Karachi

Copper objects, Mohenjodaro, National Museum, Karachi

Gamesmen, Mohenjodaro, National Museum, Karachi

61

Bronze utensils, Harappa Museum

Seals, Harappa, National Museum, Karachi.

Toys, Mohenjodaro, National Museum, Karachi

Minor objects, Mohenjodaro, National Museum, Karachi

Charred wheat, Mohenjodaro, National Museum, Karachi

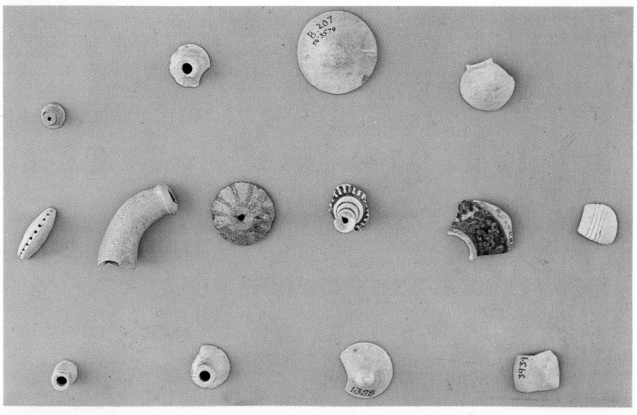

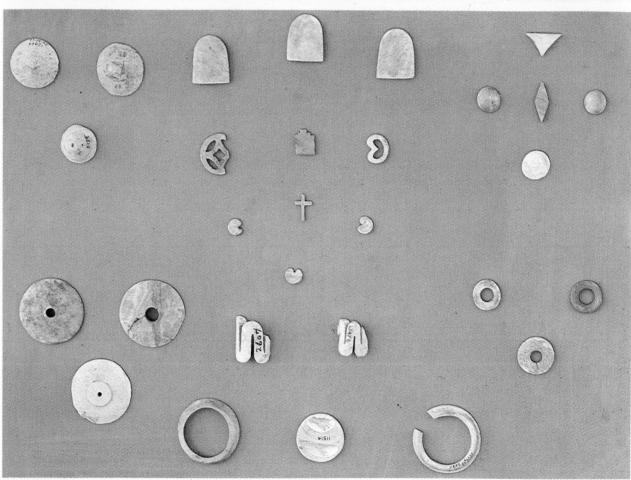

Shell objects, Harappa Museum

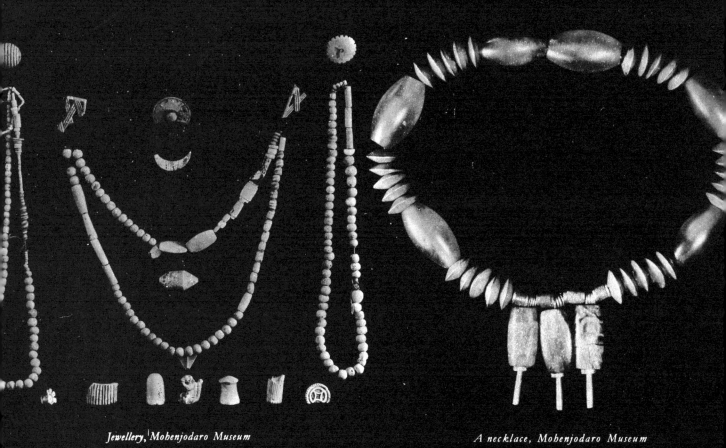

Jewellery, Mohenjodaro Museum

A necklace, Mohenjodaro Museum

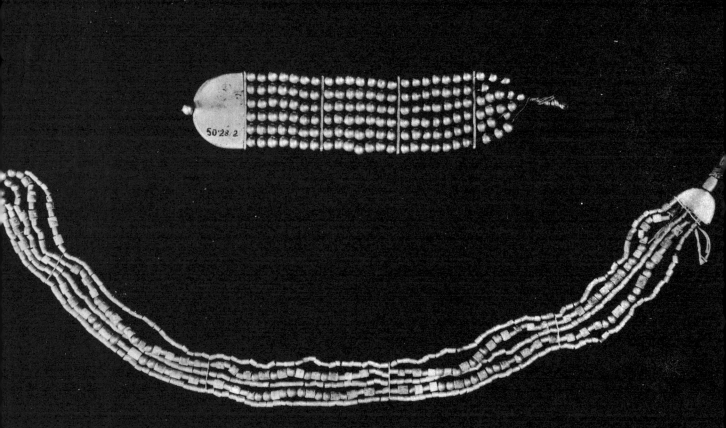

Stone and gold bead-necklaces, Mohenjodaro, National Museum, Karachi

Skeletons unearthed in a room, Mohenjodaro

Granary, Mohenjodaro

Grave Culture of Dir and Swat

DISCOVERY of a Grave culture in Dir and Swat will go a long way in throwing light on the dark period of Pakistan's cultural history between the end of the Indus Valley culture in C. 1500 B.C. and the beginning of the historic period during the Achaemenian rule in the 6th century B.C. Mythological and Sanskrit literary traditions attributed the destruction of Indus culture to the Aryans who are yet to be identified with archaeological evidence.

But the Grave culture of Dir and Swat has opened up two periods—the Bronze and the Iron Age in the cultural heritage of Pakistan. It is so named because it presents a pattern of living in the Gandhara region as evidenced by the distribution of graves spread over a large area. This culture is fundamentally different from the Indus culture and has little relation to the village culture of Baluchistan.

The Grave culture of Dir and Swat, though originated in the Bronze Age and continued into that of the Iron, represents a different phenomenon of history and is apparently linked with another folk-movement that shows strong connections with Northern Iran and Central Asia. The authors of this culture introduced the Bronze Age on the west of the Indus and ushered in an era of plain pottery tradition, as opposed to the painted pottery of the Indus Civilization. The plain pottery is seen in grey and red ware of which the plain grey ware is the harbinger of this culture.

The people of this culture mostly settled on the hill slopes beginning from the foot hills to the brink of the nearby flowing rivers and streams. The architecture was based on stone masonry, used without mortar. Large stone slabs were sometimes used as floor in the graves or to make box-like graves. No decorative element has been in the architecture.

The Grave culture represents three main burial ritual practices: (i) inflexed burial (ii) urn burial after cremation and (iii) fractional and multiple burials.

The religious life of this people still remains a mystery because of the absence of any statuary or sculpture except a few terracotta male and female figurines. These figurines show cross-band on the body but without any elaborate head-dress although

A grave with burial pottery, Swat Museum

they wear a necklace of circlets. These figurines are thought to have had some totemic significance. This totemic idea is also represented on visage urns relating to the burials with the mouth, nose, eyes and eyebrows thus representing a human face. A number of graves particularly in the last period show double burial representing male and female bodies.

The small finds and pottery discovered in the graves give us some detail about the people. Pottery forms include cooking pots, bowls-on-stand, tall drinking vases and goblets. Drinking vessels are usually in grey ware. The grey drinking vessels are a dominant feature in the graves.

The metal objects are very important in defining this culture. Apart from gold and silver, copper was the chief metal used in the first two periods. Iron came in use only in third period. Iron smithery was well advanced but weapons such as spear-heads do not show well formed mid-ribs. However, the metal technology was the dominant factor in the life of this people.

Among the small finds, long pins made of bronze, having a variety of head tops, are important. Other finds consist of ivory pins, eye-needles for stitching garments, antimony rods of ivory, iron spoons and spear-heads etc., pendants, ear-rings and finger-rings. Beads, both of precious stone and terracotta, were also in use.

On the whole the grave materials introduce to us a rapidly developing culture. The development in the three different periods is remarkable and their rapid move throughout the region is nonetheless striking. In contrast with the Indus Civilization, which was rather static through the centuries, this Grave culture was fast growing not only by borrowing materials but also by developing new forms in the course of evolution. This development is best seen in the changing form of the pottery.

Now a genuine question comes as to who were the author of this Grave culture? Archaeology has produced here material for two waves of invasion of the plain grey ware culture, the first associated with bronze and the second with iron. This culture is different from the Indus Valley Civilization. Anthropologically, these graves have brought forth two groups of western people, the proto-Europoid and the Mediterranean among whom the first group is predominant in Period I graves and the second group in Period III graves. These people are different from those buried in the Harappa cemeteries. At about the same time, literary history has produced materials about a people who called themselves Aryans and lived, in the first instance, in the land of the Sapta Sindhu and, in the second stage, spread out into the upper Ganges Valley as evidenced by the occurrence of Painted Grey Ware.

All these coincidences occurred between the end of the Indus Civilization and the beginning of the historic period in the 6th century B.C. There is thus a strong basis for the appearance of the hypothetical Aryans in history.

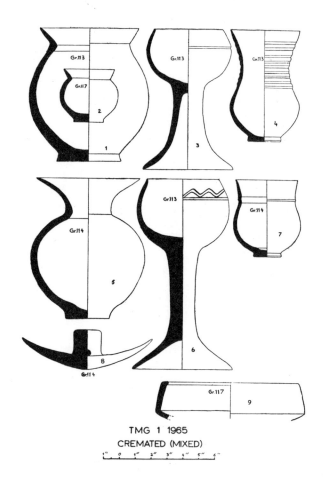

Grave culture pottery, Dir and Swat

Buddhist Period

MONASTERY AND STUPA ARCHITECTURE

ANCIENT Gandhara, the valley of Peshawar with the adjacent hilly regions of Swat and Buner, Dir and Bajaur, was one of the earliest centres of Buddhist religion and culture following the rule of the Mauryan Emperor, Ashoka, in the 3rd century B.C. The name "Gandhara" first occurs in the Rigveda, which is usually identified with the north-west frontier region, extending from Taxila on the east to Jalalabad on the west. More detailed information is, however, available in the accounts of the celebrated Chinese pilgrim, Hiuen Tsang, who visited the Buddhist sites in Gandhara in the early 7th century A.C.

The historic period of Pakistan in fact began in this region as early as the 6th century B.C. when, with the extension of the Achaemenid power towards the east, under Darius I, Gandhara became his twentieth satrapy. Then came the impact of Alexander's invasion in 327 B.C., but about 320 B.C. the region was consolidated into the Mauryan Empire of Chandragupta. The second century B.C. opened with the re-appearance of the Bactrian Greeks in the political arena of Gandhara which is amply evidenced by the discovery of their coins. By the first century B.C., the Greeks were supplanted by the Scytho-Parthians who were, in turn, over-run by the Kushans in the 1st and 2nd centuries A.C. It was the peace and prosperity of the Kushan rule which lay at the root of the development of the famous Buddhist art and architecture of Gandhara. Its prosperity declined after the invasion of the White Huns of Central Asia in the fifth century A.C.

The region of Gandhara, which had been a great centre of Buddhist culture since the 3rd century B.C., was at its zenith during the rule of Kanishka in the 1st-2nd century A.C. Buddhist sages made Gandhara a sacred region by compiling texts associating the local sites with the previous births of the Buddha. Many stupas were built in the region and numerous monastic establishments grew up.

The architectural activities of Gandhara occupy the same prominent position as its fascinating art. A number of architectural features show the influence of the western world, but whatever might be their forms, the initial inspiration is based on local elements. The basic tendency of the upward movement of Gandhara architecture was an expression of the deeply mystical attitude of Buddhist thought. Pavements in coloured glass, polychrome stucco and coloured plaster were intended to give liveliness and luminosity to the structures in which they were installed. This aesthetic technique is one of the fundamental elements of the Gandhara school which has endured through the centuries because of its intimate connection with Buddhism.

Imposing Buddhist architectural complexes are the most common forms in Gandhara. Plastic decorations, which in other areas of the sub-continent had been limited to the balustrades and gateways, was applied to the body of the stupas. The hemispherical stupa form, with or without the drum, was developed into a more elevated structure by the insertion of one or more cylindrical elements. The stupa gradually approached a tower form that was later used extensively in China. Sometime the drum rested on a podium. The series of cylindrical elements or drums were multiplied and stupas became such full structures that they seemed veritable pagodas to the Chinese pilgrims who saw them. The stupas had either a round drum or square structure on a base. The best examples of the round drum are Dharmarajika and Mohra Moradu at Taxila, Jamalgarhi in Mardan and Butkara in Swat State.

Originally the stupa was a sepulchre for the dead. In the course of time, this repository became an object of worship and, with increasing reverence, the simple, round drum assumed greater prominence and proportion. It developed into a grand hemispherical dome which housed within it the relics. According to the Buddhist practice the stupas were divided into four categories: (a) relic, (b) commemorative, (c) votive and (d) model stupas. The relic stupas originally contained the relics of the Buddha or his disciples. Later on, stupas were erected to commemorate some events of the life of the Buddha or some great saint. In due course, the places of the relic and commemorative stupas became centres of pilgrimage where the Buddhist devotees built votive stupas as a work of

Sleeping musician, Taxila Museum

great religious merit. Before the representation of the image of the Buddha, model stupas carved on stone reliefs indicated his death. This type had symbolical meaning.

When the stupa was looked upon as an object of homage, it was fenced off by a railing such as we find at Sanchi and Bharhut in India. This practice was not followed in Gandhara. Here, the solid conical structure was raised on a high base, round or square in plan. The base was decorated with sculptures depicting various scenes in the Buddha's life. Sometimes, a screen wall was added to protect the sculptures. Rows of sculptures also adorned the main body of the stupa drum. The stupa structure consists of a base, a cylindrical drum, and a hemispherical dome superimposed by seven disc-shaped umbrellas one above the other, supported on an upright staff which rests firmly inside a square box called the *harmika*. The *harmika* contains the relics. The stupa in this delicate and imposing form possessed a noble height and a dominating look. It is this concept of the stupa which became a symbol of worship in Buddhist art. The round shaped stupa needed an apse-like projection at one end and such an apsidal arrangement exists at Sirkap near Taxila. Later on was evolved the true Gandhara style of erecting the stupa on a square base in the middle of monastic courtyards as at Takht-i-Bahi. With this evolution, a compromise was reached between the purely symbolic idea of a stupa and the stupa decorated with sculptures for teaching the lessons of the Buddha. This change was in keeping with the spirit of the Mahayana school of Buddhism in Gandhara.

Excavations in the Gandhara region, particularly at Taxila, have brought to light the remains of three ancient settlements, namely, the Bhir Mound, Sirkap and Sirsukh and a large number of Buddhist stupas and monasteries. The earliest settlement of Bhir Mound stand on a small plateau near the western end of the valley of Taxila. The layout of the settlement is haphazard, the streets for the most part being narrow and tortuous and the house-plans are irregular. According to local tradition, the Bhir Mound is the most ancient of all the sites at Taxila and this has been confirmed by excavations which indicate that this settlement had been thrice destroyed and thrice rebuilt before the Bactrian Greeks built a new city at Sirkap. The four successive settlements on the Bhir Mound represent a cultural sequence from the 6th century B.C. to the 1st century B.C. As the Mound stood at the entrance to the southern part of the valley, it was natural that the Dharmarajika stupa, the earliest of all the Buddhist monuments at Taxila, should be erected here and that other Buddhist monasteries and stupas should afterwards stand in the

same area which thus became sacred to Buddhism.

The Sirkap city, built by the Bactrian Greeks in the beginning of the 2nd century B.C., occupies the extreme western spurs of the Hathial ridges together with the small well-defined plateau on their northern side. Excluding these suburbs, the Sirkap defence wall was nearly 3.5 miles in circumference and was built of solid, coursed stone rubble. In accordance with the Hellenistic principles of defence, the defence wall included within its perimeter a considerable area of hilly ground as well as a well-laid out city on the Greek chess-board pattern, with streets cutting one another at right angles and regularly aligned blocks of buildings. Notwithstanding that the settlement was several times destroyed and rebuilt and that many changes were made in individual buildings, this Greek lay-out remained well preserved down to the end of the 1st century A.C.

The third city, called Sirsukh, is situated to the north-east of the Lundi stream. It dates from the early Kushana times and is laid out in the traditional manner of Central Asian cities of that period with which the Kushans were familiar. Its plan is roughly a parallelogram with a perimeter of about 3 miles. Like Sirkap, it is defended by a massive stone wall, but the wall is faced with "diaper" masonry instead of coursed rubble, and strengthened on the outside by semi-circular bastions. It also possessed a suburb on its western side.

Besides the remains of these three settlements there are numbers of isolated monuments, mainly stupas and monasteries, scattered about the valley of Taxila. The remains are specially numerous in the southern half of the valley, the oldest and most conspicuous of them being the imposing Dharmarajika Stupa and monastery. As regards the origin of this stupa, it is said that it was built by Ashoka to house the relic of the Buddha. The stupa is circular in plan with its drum resting on a raised terrace, which was ascended by four flights of steps, one at each of the cardinal points. Its diameter including the terrace and the steps is 150 ft. from east to west and 146 ft. 6 inches from north to south and the existing height is about 45 ft. The core is of rough masonry strengthened by sixteen walls, from 3 ft. to 5 ft. in thickness, radiating irregularly from the centre. The terrace is faced with an early type semi-ashlar masonry. The outer facing of the stupa is of ponderous limestone blocks with chiselled Kanjur stone let in between them for the moulding and pilasters, the whole having once been finished with a coating of lime plaster and paint.

The ornamental stone carving on the face of the stupa, above the berm, is best preserved on the eastern side. Its most distinguishing features consist in the boldness of its moulding and the design of its

Bird's eye view of Sirkap site and the Taxila valley, Taxila

Dipankara Jataka, Swat Museum

niches which are framed alternately by trefoil arches and portals with sloping jambs and separated from one another by Corinthian pilasters. These niches once held figures of the Buddha or of the Bodhisattva in relief. The same kind of decoration is also found on smaller stupas on this site belonging to the 4th and 5th centuries A.C. It seems possible, it was first erected in the reign of Ashoka in the 3rd century B.C. That it was already standing at the time of the early Saka King, Maues and Azes, is proved by the circle of small stupas around it, which are contemporary with those rulers.

The raised terrace and the open passage around the foot of the stupa served as the procession path round which it was customary for the faithful to walk, keeping the stupa always on the right hand.

The most remarkable find from the Dharmarajika stupa was that of a reliquary in one of the side-chapels, containing a silver scroll with a Kharoshthi inscription recording that the associated relics were those of the Buddha himself. It also gives the date of the enshrinement and mentions the place-name Takshasila (Taxila). It is worthy of note that the writer describes himself as a Bactrian.

The great complex of stupa buildings at Dharmarajika, must have been dominated by the moulded, sculptured and painted stucco which covered the rough masonry.

The best example of stucco ornament is provided by the stupas and monastery at Jaulian, three miles east-north-east of Sirkap. The group includes the square base of a large stupa, surrounded by a number of stucco votive stupas and over-looking a small court framed with shrines. From this court, a short flight of steps leads to the court of cells, an assembly hall, kitchen and refectory. Each cell was lighted by a narrow loop set high in the wall and was provided with lamp-niches and storage-pots. Stone-stairs led to the upper storey. Here and there between the cells were wall-niches containing sculptures. At Jaulian, we are presented with a well-preserved Buddhist establishment of about 400-450 A.C.

Another significant feature of the monastery plan at Jaulian is the space allotted for the assembly hall and refectory. In its earlier days, the Buddhist monastery had been primarily a house of monks who sustained themselves individually by begging. Their economy must have been reduced to a minimum and monastery was in essence a focus for priests and devotees engaged selflessly in teaching and learning the Buddhist tenets. Gradually, the merit acquired by patronizing the monk or his monastery assumed something more than a spiritual value, and substantial gifts and endowments from the aspiring layman turned the simple monk into a man of property. The monasteries became great land-owners, the begging bowl was replaced by the well-lined refectory and this took the form of a hall to which were now added kitchen and store houses. Jaulian illustrates structurally a mature phase of this development.

Besides these Buddhist monuments, the Fire Temple at Taxila deserves special mention. At Jandial, less than half a mile from the north gate of Sirkap, there are the remains of a building which resemble a Greek temple not only in plan but also in the fact that the two columns of the portico are in Greek style. In two respects, however, the building is different from its western analogues. Instead of the surrounding colonade, it had a continuous outside wall pierced by window-like openings and behind the main shrine was a solid platform approached from the back by steps. This was presumably carried up to some sort of a tower. Sir John Marshall conjectured from this evidence and also from the absence of images, that the temple belonged to the Zoroastrians. It enabled the faithful to offer prayers in praise of the Sun, Moon and all other elements which led their thoughts to Nature's God. On this supposition, the main shrine would presumably have contained a fire-altar. The building is ascribed, by the character of its masonry, to the Scytho-Parthian period of about 1st century B.C. to 1st century A.C.

Shahji-ki-Dheri, Peshawar

The Buddhist establishments of Taxila were rivalled and sometimes out-done by many other Buddhist monuments particularly in and about the Peshawar Valley. In the south-eastern outskirts of Peshawar city, stood the famous stupa, popularly known as Shahji-ki-Dheri, that commemorated the conversion of King Kanishka to Buddhism. According to the Chinese pilgrim, Hiuen Tsang, it towered above a base built in five stages to a total height of 550 feet with a super-structure of 25 gilded copper discs. Excavations revealed that the walls of the stupa were of stone diaper masonry and retained traces of stucco decoration consisting of standing Buddhas between pilasters. An interesting and valuable discovery was that of fragmentary brick bearing a Kharoshthi inscription.

In the centre, amidst the massive radiating walls, which formed the structural framework of the stupa was unearthed a relic-chamber. In one of its corners was found the famous Kanishka relic casket, made of copper alloy. On its lid are small figures, in the round, of a seated Buddha flanked by two Bodhisattvas. In relief, round the upper part of the cylinder, is a frieze of flying geese: below is the main frieze with a figure of King Kanishka standing in front of an undulating garland supported by garland-bearers and framing

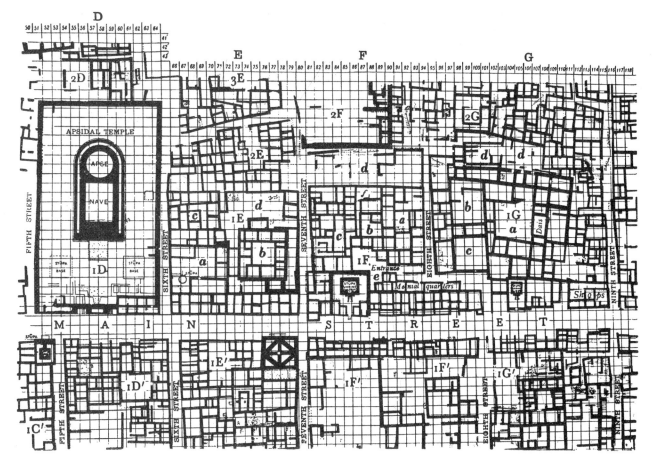

Sirkap: plan of Blocks D, E, F, G.

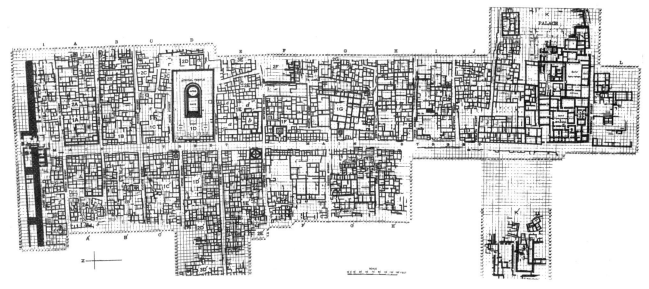

Sirkap: plan of excavations in the lower city showing the second (Parthian) stratum.

Bhallar Stupa, Taxila

Terracotta head of an old man,
National Museum, Karachi.

General view of Sirkap site, Taxila

Dharmarajika Stupa, Taxila

Buddhist Monastery, Takht-i-Bahi

General view of stupas, Butkara, Swat.

Kanishka's Relic Casket, Peshawar Museum 82

Bird's eye view of Mohra Moradu monastery, Taxila

Fasting Buddha, Lahore Museum

84

Mohra Moradu monastery, Taxila

Buddha in Dhyana Mudra, National Museum, Karachi

Roma or Minerva, Lahore Museum

Birth of the Buddha, National Museum, Karachi

demi-figures of votaries. On the lid and sides is a punctured inscription in Kharoshthi which twice mentions the name of Kanishka and concludes with the name of the master mason, Agishala.

Within the copper reliquary lay a six sided crystal container with three fragments of bone, undoubtedly relics of the Buddha. The reliquary is now one of the prized treasures of the Peshawar Museum.

Takht-i-Bahi

The best preserved monument in the Peshawar region is the Buddhist monastery of Takht-i-Bahi, standing on a rocky ridge about 10 miles north-east of Mardan. The building complex includes a stupa and a monastic quadrangle. Towards the west of quadrangle is a large square assembly hall. The main stupa-court is flanked by other courtyards with votive stupas, and Buddhist sculptures in situ.

Sculptures in stone and stucco found in large number indicate the importance of this site. The most interesting features of the building complex are the design and arrangement of small shrines which surround the main stupa-court. These shrines, containing votive stupa and sculptures stood on a sculptured podium and were crowned alternately with stupa-like finials and gabled chaityas, all forming an ensemble without parallel.

Buddhist Remains at Chanaka Dheri

The mound of Chanaka Dheri near Shahbaz Garhi, in the district of Mardan, revealed building remains of a Buddhist religious character. These structures were built in the style of small diaper masonry so common in the Gandhara region. The massive building at Chanaka Dheri stood on a plinth 15 feet high

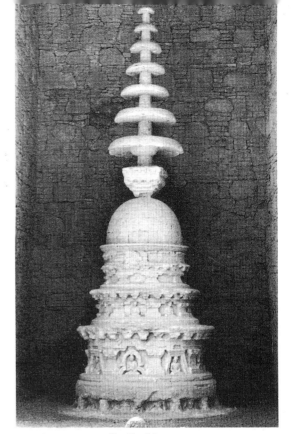
Miniature stupa, Taxila Museum

and was provided with rooms which had wooden door frames. One of the rooms contained a large rectangular bench placed in the middle and plastered with lime on top. The walls were also coated with thick lime plaster. Similar monastic establishments were also brought to light at Tharelli and some other sites in the area.

Buddhist Remains of Swat

Swat, the ancient Buddhist land of 'Udyana', is very rich in archaeological wealth and excavations conducted at a number of sites by the Italian Archaeological Mission, in recent times, have revealed innumerable Buddhist remains of considerable importance. Thousands of fine specimens of Gandhara art, from this area, show the different stages of its development and evolution. Excavations at Butkara, near Mingora, revealed a large and imposing central stupa surrounded by more than 200 votive stupas. Here, hundreds of sculptured slabs and panels of Gandhara art carved in green schist, depicting the life story of the Buddha, have been discovered. They originally embellished the plinths of the stupas. From several minor stupas, relic caskets, intact with the inner golden container, have been recovered. The excavated remains have been identified with the monastery of 'Talo' mentioned by the Chinese pilgrim Song-Yun. The establishment was destroyed by a disastrous flood in the 3rd century A.C.

Udegram, the Ora of the Greeks, was the principal city at the time of Alexander's invasion. Within

Double headed eagle shrine, Taxila

Stucco bust of an Atlant, Taxila Museum

Close view of front face, Dharmarajika Stupa, Taxila

Close view of double-headed eagle shrine, Taxila

the Udegram town-site, a considerable area of the ancient town with a network of streets and lanes and blocks of habitation, associated with abundant objects of every day use, has been uncovered. The houses are built on a uniform plan, with a small entrance opening into a courtyard serving the residential part. Along the streets are rows of single rooms which were in all probability shops and hence the area is called the 'Bazar'. Destruction of the town and the 'Bazar' of Udegram seem to have been caused by frequent floods. The evidence of coins, minor objects and pottery indicates that this city rose into prominence about the 4th century B.C. and lasted to the 4th century A.C. It remained under the influence of the Indo-Greeks, Sakas, Parthians, and Kushans after the invasion of Alexander.

The rich material comprising the stucco, terracotta and stone sculptures and other minor works of art discovered from Swat sites certainly make a noteworthy contribution to the classification of Gandhara art and help significantly in the reconstruction of the history of the Gandhara region.

Among other Buddhist monuments of importance in West Pakistan, the Shaikan Dheri in Peshawar district, the stupas of Mohenjodaro, Mirpur Khas, Thul Mir Rukan near Moro, Depar Ghangro near Brahmanabad, Sudheran-jo-dharo near Tando Mohammad Khan, and the one near Jarak, are noteworthy.

GANDHARA ART

Gandhara art is one of the most prized treasures of Pakistan. It represents a phase of cultural efflorescence which was the result of the fervent zeal and religious consciousness of Buddhism that had affected the life of the people. It is this religious awakening that inspired the creation of Gandhara art and one cannot miss the noble personality of the Buddha and his message when viewing this art in its various forms.

Gandhara art derived inspiration from local traditions with a touch of alien influence. The art designated as Graeco-Buddhist or Romano-Buddhist is certainly a misleading term, since it implies derivation from the Greek or Roman art traditions. It has, however, little affinity with the Greek or Roman art and is much more akin to the traditional art of the land where it took its birth and developed into a mature form.

During the span of one thousand years, from the time of Persian conquest to the invasion of the White Huns from 600 B.C. to the 5th century A.C., the Gandhara region prospered under such foreign rulers

90

as the Achaemenians, the Greeks, the Bactrians, the Scytho-Parthians and the Kushans who all left their influence in one form or the other. In spite of these successive changes of ruler, the bulk of the population remained faithful to the culture of the soil. The greatest unifying force was, no doubt, the Buddhist faith which the Gandharans had adopted during the reign of Ashoka, the Buddhist Constantine. Buddhism provided an unbreakable bond to the Gandharans, with the other parts of the Indus region. The artistic manifestations of Buddhism, as evolved in Gandhara, materially strengthened these bonds and influenced deeply the later Buddhist art of Central Asia, China, Japan and other far eastern countries. Its birth and development is of later date than the early period art sculptures of the Mauryas. It grew and flourished independently; it remained distinctly indigenous with its subject matter and other characteristic features but it is primarily a religious art serving the Buddhist faith. Sculptures and paintings on stupas and monasteries depicted important tenets of Buddhism which lent themselves to pictorial representation.

Among the Gandhara art treasures, sculptures form the most important group for their individuality and technique. The material chiefly used by the sculptors was a kind of blue schist. Where such stone proved rare, images were made in stucco or plaster. In a later period, when mechanical reproduction became common, stucco and plaster sculptures were employed

An ascetic, Lahore Museum

Birth of the Buddha in stucco, Peshawar Museum

91

The Buddha, Peshawar, National Museum, Karachi.

Terracotta votive plaque representing a male and a female figure standing side by side and holding hands
Squatting figure on a cushion holding animal in carve of left arm
Plaque with standing figure of a female deity in relief. Pinkish red terracotta. Taxila Museum

extensively for the embellishment of religious buildings.

The chief patrons of Gandhara art were the Kushans, and the reason of their patronage is not difficult to understand. Their conversion to Buddhism and their patronage of local art traditions, were part of a policy designed to maintain their authority in the conquered land. In their coins they also patronized deities of different religions.

Buddhism, in origin, was not a religion but a philosophy of life. The Buddha, the Enlightened One, according to the orthodox school, was not a god but an inspired teacher who preached the Middle Path between indulgence and asceticism, and sought an ultimate deliverance from the sufferings of the cycles of life by supreme detachment. Later, by a more progressive school of thought, Buddha was increasingly regarded as a divine being to whom prayer might be offered. These divergent opinions resulted in the formation of two schools called Hinayana and Mahayana. The Mahayana school of Buddhism attained maturity in the Gandhara region in the 1st-2nd century A.C. during the rule of the Kushan king Kanishka.

In artistic expression, the outstanding difference between these two schools of Buddhism was that, in

Terracotta head of Bodhisattva, Taxila,
National Museum, Karachi

the Hinayana practices, the Buddha alone was represented either by a symbol or in person. His presence was symbolized by a throne, a foot-print, an umbrella, a riderless horse, the Bodhi-tree, a head-dress or shoes surrounded by a tumultuous masses and there was no central figure. In the Mahayana school, on the other hand, the figure of the divine Buddha along with those of the Bodhisattvas controls the assembly and is the focus of its composition. Both iconographically and aesthetically this change was revolutionary.

The Gandhara school is credited with the first representation of the Buddha in human form. The portrayal of Sakyamuni, in his human shape, rather than as a symbol, is probably linked with the emergence of a devotional cult of Buddhism at the time of Kanishka's Great council.

In addition to the introduction of the Buddha image, the Gandhara school is also to be credited with the presentation of the Bodhisattva. His images were all intended as representations of the Buddha

Head of a female in stucco, Khyber Pass, Peshawar Museum

Amorous couple, Swat Museum

in his princely state before he attained the enlightenment. The Bodhisattvas in Gandhara art are shown wearing turbans, jewellery and thin muslin skirts, a dress of the Kushans. The representation of Bodhisattva figures is an interesting religious development which took place after the death of the Buddha.

Gandhara art derives its name from the ancient geographic region in which it originated and developed. However, its art traditions did not remain confined to one particular locality, but spread northward across the Kabul river in Afghanistan and also to Central Asia. The artistic activities of Tibet, China, India and other Far Eastern countries amply bear testimony to the Gandhara art influence. Throughout this wide belt of influence, Gandhara art is distinctly recognized for its own individuality, unity of content and the ideal of the Gandhara social life which gave it birth.

In Gandhara art, the Buddha figure, though dominating, is not the only representation. It depicts vividly and effectively every day life of Gandhara in a vast panoramic composition such as the movement of the monks in their flowing yellow dress walking silently; the royal chariot of the king who pays homage to the Buddha; the grass-cutter in all humility making his humble offering; the ploughman furrowing the field in traditional manner; the muscular

Amorous couple, Swat Museum

wrestlers grappling; and scenes depicting couples making love and drinking wine. All these and many other events are represented in the manner they were observed in the daily life of the people. Even the personality of the Buddha and many incidents of his life are produced in such a manner as if they tell the truth of life which the Buddha attained.

The region of Gandhara has occupied a pivotal position in the movement of people since antiquity. It proved to be a veritable home of various peoples who settled down here, merged in the local populace and regenerated with the evolution of Gandhara art and culture. The settlers still retained some of their own cultural traits which inevitably influenced the life of the local people. Even today, we witness the

Worship of the head dress of Bodhisattva, Peshawar Museum

Votive stupas at Panr, Swat

Lion in stone before the main stupa, Butkara, Swat

The Buddha in Dharma-Chakra Mudra,
National Museum, Karachi

Fire altar, Jandial, Taxila

The Buddha with an ascetic, National Museum, Karachi

Buddha in Dhyana
Mudra in stucco,
Taxila Museum

Headless draped female, Taxila Museum

Central Asian trousers and caps worn by the male Pathans and the long loose flowing skirts used by the Waziri ladies. The representation of royal ladies in Gandhara art in classical tunic does not necessarily suggest the import of this dress from the classical world. This, and many other types of dress and the ways of living, must have been the legacy of the Greeks who ruled here for about two hundred years before the rise of the Kushans. These elements integrated in Gandhara art under the force of rapidly moving changes brought by Buddhism in this region.

At the time of the introduction of Buddhism in Gandhara, the Buddhist missionaries brought some cultural trends from outside, but Buddhism could establish its root in the new home only when it compromised with local aspirations and the new strains of life that were coming in the wake of migration of peoples. All the cultural traits found in Gandhara point to the formation of national concepts of the ancient people of that region. It was the integration of this national force which led to the fruition of the Gandhara art and culture.

Some art critics see through their eyes the origin of Gandhara art in the Greek or Roman traditions. If this point is carefully examined with reference to the stratified levels of excavations conducted at different sites in Gandhara, the Greek or Roman influence would prove to be mere beginning of a new art as a result of fresh relationship with Western Asia. It is an admitted fact that the glory of Gandhara art reached its zenith in the days of the Kushans whose vast empire was not certainly devoid of artists. That the Kushans did possess such creative people, is clear from the art of the Mathura and Gandhara

Pedimental slab showing worship of the bowl and the Buddha in Abhaya Mudra, Peshawar Museum

schools. If the Kushans wanted to commission craftsmen from outside to develop their art, there is no reason why they should not have imported them from among the Mathura artists who were readily available and were imbued with the spirit of Buddhism. The theory of hired craftsmen from the Greek or Roman lands, for the development of Gandhara art, is at once nullified when we think that the creation of such a deep religious art as that seen in Gandhara, was developed by the hired craftsmen who had no feeling for Buddhism, no experience of Buddhist life and no heart for appreciating Buddhist truth.

SCULPTURE

The concepts of Gandhara art, especially the treatment of its sculptures, are different from those seen in various schools of Indian art. The Gandhara specimens have a direct appeal with an individuality of their own. There is a singular unity throughout in their form and composition for which the art is a distinct school. The Hellenic romanticism or Roman individuality is definitely missing in the portrayal of Gandhara sculpture. In Gandhara the individual is a part of humanity. The image of the Buddha in Gandhara is an ideal human who is above common man but still not a god. He is a participant in the human activities of the world and yet at the same time he is an embodiment of moral lessons bearing a youthful face unaffected by age or worldly affliction. The Buddha figure with two-fold dress, over-

The Buddha visiting ascetic Asita, Peshawar Museum

Kunala stupa, Taxila

head protruberance termed Ushnisha, curl of hair between eye-brows called Urna, and appearing in different poses is quite distinct from the well-known Mathura type. It is this touch of humanity that has been represented in the reliefs depicting the incidents from the early life of the Buddha.

Among the Bodhisattva group of sculptures, the Bodhisattva Maitreya from Mohra Moradu monastery near Taxila standing on a pedestal is a unique piece. The figure wears two garments, one tied at the waist and falling in graceful folds to the ankles and the other draped around the upper part of the body. The garments are arranged in such a way that they cover

Bodhisattva, Taxila Museum

A devotee holding the flame of Dharma, National Museum, Karachi

the right side except the arm, shoulder and upper chest. The hair is tied above in a loop while it is bound below by strings of beads with a cylindrical clasp in front. Save for a moustache the face is clean shaved. The left hand is lost and from the mortice in the right fore-arm it is evident that the missing portion was originally a separate piece. The figure wears sandals with jewelled lacings. The Urna is represented as a small circular projection. Of the halo only traces remain.

The Buddhist stupa, Mankiyala

View of the Fire temple, Jandial, Taxila

A Yakshi, Swat Museum

Bodhisattva, National Museum, Karachi

Harpocrates in bronze, Taxila Museum

A female torso, Lahore Museum

The method of representing the Buddha stories in a series of separate panels is a distinct break from the practice of continuous narration that was invariably employed in the ancient Indian schools. Of the scenes from the Buddha's life, one depicting his First Sermon is an outstanding example. Here the haloed Buddha is seated on a grass-strewn throne and holds the hem of his robe with his left hand while he touches the Wheel of Law with his right hand. The wheel rests on the three points of a Tri-ratna supported by a dwarf pillar. Flanking the throne are two couchant deer. An unusual feature of the left hand side of the Buddha is the presence of Indra, haloed but defaced, while Brahma, likewise haloed and in the guise of a Brahman novice, occupies the corres-

ponding position on the Buddha's right. A bearded Vajrapani with fly-whisk in right hand and a vajra in left stands to the right of Brahma while in the left foreground two monks are seated on low, circular, grass-strewn seats. The right side of the panel is lost and of the other three monks, only traces of one and his seat remain. A spirited haloed flying Deva with flower offering in left hand fills the upper left corner. This piece is presently displayed in the Taxila Museum.

Another relief depicts the visit of Indra to the Buddha in Indrashala cave. The panel is divided horizontally into two compartments by a balustrade in the form of a railing. In the lower, the Buddha is seen seated in meditation in a cave with his hands hidden in his robe. Outside the cave on his left stands the haloed Indra, with his head-dress and clasped hands. An interesting feature is the presence of a haloed Brahma on the other side of the cave, shown in an attitude of adoration.

A large number of stone friezes depicting the incidents of the life of the Buddha have been unearthed at various sites in Pakistan. His birth as Bodhisattva is shown in the seventh heaven where he is implored to descend on to earth to show men the right way to salvation. The Bodhisattva selected Queen Maya of the Shakya family in Nepal as his mother. After descending on earth he entered the womb of the Queen as a white elephant while she was dreaming of conception. Ten months later he was born out of the right side of his mother with 32 marks of greatness in the Lumbini garden under a Shala tree. He was named Siddhartha.

When he grew up, King Shuddhodana, his father, was prophesised by the Brahmin astrologer that the Prince would either retire from the mundane life to become a Buddha or stay in profane life to become a powerful ruler. In order to prevent the renunciation of the prince, King Shuddhodana provided him with all the worldly enjoyments.

Prince Siddhartha married to Yashodhara, a girl of a noble family, led a happy life. While making pleasure trips, the Prince met successively an old man, an ill man, a funeral procession and a mellow mendicant walking along in quiet temper. On seeing these scenes, the prince suddenly recognized the sadness and sorrows of life and decided to leave the palace in search of higher perception.

All efforts to prevent him leaving princely life were in vain. At the age of twenty nine he left his wife, while she was sleeping, with the help of gods on horse back at night and began his wandering in search of enlightenment. He met learned teachers, but their methods did not satisfy the Bodhisattva in the attainment of his goal. Even the hardest asceticism which he practised for six years and which reduced him to skeleton did not bring him any way nearer to his quest for enlightenment. He realized the fruitlessness of this hard experiment and went to Bodhgaya. There under the Bodhi-tree he absorbed himself deeply in meditation. Mara, the personification of profane principle and sensuality for fear of losing his worldly position if the Bodhisattva attained enlightenment, rushed with his demon force to the Bodhi-tree and attacked the Bodhisattva.

The latter remained unperturbed in meditation and even ignored the sensual temptation of Mara's beautiful daughters. Mara was thus defeated in his attempts. At last in a full moon-light the Prince attained enlightenment and became a Buddha or the Enlightened One. Full of delight came all the gods out of heaven to do homage to the Buddha.

The Enlightened One decided to teach the Law to the mankind as requested by god Brahma. So in the Deer-Park of Benares, the Buddha preached for the first time to five disciples. Then up to the age of 80 he wandered preaching through the length and breadth of the country and found many confessors, monks, nuns, lay brothers and sisters for his new religion. Often he had to demonstrate his miraculous powers to prove his mastery over water and fire, and over space and time.

At the age of 80 he fell ill and Ananda, his favourite disciple prepared the last resting place for him between two Shala-trees near Kushinagara. There he entered in deep meditation while lying and left into entire Nirvana. The nobles of Kushinagara arranged obsequies over six days and burnt the mortal relics

A bejewelled lady, Swat Museum

on the seventh day. The bones were later on placed in Stupas.

The events of the life of the great Master were carved in stone and stucco by the Gandhara artists with meticulous precision.

In Gandhara art the representations of the Buddha and Bodhisattva are easily distinguishable. The Buddha figure is based on the literary traditions, such as the appearance of the excrescence on the head and the curly formation between the eye-brows. It is doubtful whether in the beginning the excrescence of the head was represented as such on purpose or whether the Buddha figure simply got a topknot which then was turned into an ushnisha. At any rate the topknot on the Buddha heads became a characteristic mark in Gandhara art.

Other favourite symbols like the wheel of law or the "three jewels" are to be found on the palm or

A Corinthian capital showing female figure, Swat Museum

A devotee, Swat Museum ▶

the sole of Buddha's foot. His gown is that of a Buddhist monk. It consists of an undergown, an over gown and a cloak. The positions of his legs and hands are of symbolic importance. In one form the right arm is lifted up showing the palm. This position is called 'the gesture of giving protection'. In another composition the Buddha is seen in deep meditation with hands placed on the upturned soles of feet resting one above the other, and palms turned up with stretched fingers.

To these two early postures, two more positions were added later on. They are the gesture of 'touching the earth' and the "setting-in-motion-the-Wheel-of-the-Law". The first posture refers to the events of enlightenment when Buddha, attacked by Mara, called on the goddess of earth to bear witness of his meritorious doings. In the sculptural representations the right hand of the Great Master touches the earth while the left hand is placed on the lap. The second

Descend of the Buddha from Traystrimsa Heaven, Swat Museum

Buddha head in stucco, Taxila Museum

attitude symbolizes how the Buddha put in motion the wheel of Law. Here both of his hands are held in a certain position in front of his chest. The nimbus is plain.

The Bodhisattva figure differs from that of the Buddha by the profane dress and princely decoration like the crown, jewels, necklaces and armlets. He is also depicted wearing a talisman chain with small boxes and ear trinklets.

In Gandhara reliefs, the Buddha is often accompanied by his tutelary genius Vajrapani or the one who holds a thunderbolt in his hand. Other divinities who generally accompany the Buddha are Indra and Brahma or sometimes Panchika and Hariti both of them are protectors of children. Other subordinate divine beings like Yakshas and Yakshis living in the woods, rocks and trees are also represented in the friezes. Among human beings, nobles, monks, Brahmans and lay devotees are depicted on the pedestals.

Besides stone reliefs the Gandhara craftsmen produced stucco and terracotta sculptures. These are endowed with deep feeling, spontaneity of modelling and are less academic in execution than the stone works. A fine series of thirty one Buddha and Bodhisattva figures carved on a wall of the main stupa at Mohra Moradu near Taxila is considered to be the best example of its kind. The wall is divided into several bays and in one of the bays the Buddha is shown in "setting-in-motion-the-Wheel-of-Law"

116

Dipankara Jataka, Swat Museum

A devotee, Taxila Museum

attitude, sitting on a lion throne and surrounded by Bodhisattvas and Devas. The dignified postures, calm expression, delicate modelling of drapery and the requisite features of the Bodhisattvas and the tender expression of the Devas render them as the finest specimen of this school. Another example from the Jaulian monastery in the same area is the centrally seated Buddha in the attitude of meditation with standing Buddhas to his right and left and two attendant figures behind. This group is not only the best preserved example of stucco sculptures but also a rare example showing the local influence. Still another striking group of figures from the same monastery is modelled, unlike others, out of clay. Here the figure of the donor with a conical cap and Parthian dress is of special interest.

The chronology of the Gandhara sculptures is a vexing problem due largely to the absence of any

A female torso, Taxila Museum

The Buddha in adamantine attitude, front and back view, Taxila Museum

definite datable material. A large number of sculptured pieces do bear inscriptions with a reckoning in years of unspecified eras. It is, however, possible now to arrive at a tentative chronology by reference to the stratified level in Gandhara region. Among the earliest examples is generally included the famous bronze reliquary of king Kanishka in the Peshawar Museum which bears a date of his early regnal year. Its style is a mixture of the local elements combined with some iconographical characters of the West, such as the garland-bearers circling the drum of the casket. The earliest Buddhas from Gandhara region, datable by inscriptions, belong to the 3rd century A.C.

It is reasonable to point out that in the early stages of Gandhara art the favourite medium for carving was the blue schist and green phyllite. In the 4th century A.C. stucco became more popular. The malleable nature of this medium made for a freedom of expression eluded the carvers of the intractable stone. The use of stucco for architectural decoration is usually traced from Western Asia and it was during the time of the Parthians in the 1st century B.C. that stucco is first employed in Gandhara.

*A Yakshi holding a lotus, front and back view,
Taxila, National Museum, Karachi*

The sculptures of Gandhara seem to confirm the testimony of the Chinese pilgrims on the predominance of the Hinayana sect of Buddhism. The subject matter of the single figures is for the most part restricted to representations of the mortal Buddha Shakyamuni, and Maitreya, the Buddha of the Future. The reliefs are devoted entirely to the illustrations of the Buddha and the legends of his earlier incarnations. Others identifiable as the Bodhisattva and reliefs with multiple Buddha images may be the earliest examples of Mahayana Buddhist sculpture. Probably in deference to local native belief, the sculptures also represented the fertility spirits of Panchika and Hariti.

Due to its political stability in the north-western regions of Pakistan and the maintenance of contacts with the west, the Gandhara art enjoyed a great longevity and monotony of expression. It is the repetition of type and techniques that a period of nearly five centuries renders any kind of chronology on a stylistic basis very difficult. However, it can be stated that the school reached the zenith of its production

A Buddha head, Peshawar Museum

and aesthetic effectiveness in the 2nd century A.C.

The disastrous invasions of the White Huns in the 5th century A.C. adversely affected the art and architecture in Gandhara. But the tradition lingered languishingly. Most of the sculptures at Butkara belong to post-Hun period. The Chinese pilgrim Hiuen Tsang's account of the ruined monasteries that he saw everywhere in the Gandhara Valley is probably an accurate description of the terrible desolation of this once flourishing Buddhist centre.

MINOR ARTS

Besides sculptures and architectural remains, the Gandhara region has produced a variety of material such as metal objects, pottery, domestic and toilet articles, jewellery, coins, inscriptions, tools and implements, and war weapons of varied importance and interest especially from Taxila and Shaikhan Dheri.

Pottery

Pottery vessels, after stone friezes, form the second major collection from Gandhara. These are mostly of utilitarian type and without much decoration. In pottery, storage jars, oil and wine vessels, flasks, waterpots, water bottles, cooking pots, surahi, handled jugs, drinking cups, bowls and saucers, pans and dishes, water condensers and lamps—all are represented. Of particular interest are a handled jug of red-buff clay and a water bottle. The jug has a squat body with a flat base and its mouth is thrown back and pinched. It has a ring handle. The water bottle

is circular in shape with one side flattened. At the top is a mouth with a short neck and two pierced lobes with grooves for cord.

Domestic pottery is so abundant that a picture of every day life of that period can be had from them. Cooking pots, jugs, ewers, drinking cups, goblets, bowls, cups, dishes, saucers, pans, basins, ladles, spoons, incense burners, all are represented with developed shapes and fine workmanship.

A female devotee in stucco, Taxila Museum

A dancer, Swat Museum

Birth of Siddhartha's horse Kanthaka, Swat Museum

Silver and bronze objects

The household objects are of two categories, silver wares and copper and bronze wares. Silverwares which are not so abundant and belong to the 1st century A.C. include jugs, goblets, bowls, cups, dishes, plates, ladles, spoons and strainers. A circular strainer with broad flat rim furnished with a ring handle is most interesting. In the second category a handled jug of copper with narrow neck, a bronze bowl with concave base and incarved sides, a bronze frying pan with a fluted handle having ram's head at the end, a goblet with carinated shoulder and a cloven-hoof spoon of beaten copper with oval bowl are well preserved specimens.

Metal Sculptures

Metal sculptures, though rare, are all solid and cast in open or piece moulds. The bronze statuette of the Childgod 'Harpocrates' is the most notable among the collections. The Childgod stands with heels almost together, wearing a long sleeve-less tunic which reaches up to the ankles and leaves the left shoulder bare. His right forefinger is raised and touches his lips, as if in silence. His left hand holds

A devotee, Swat Museum

The Buddha, Swat Museum

some indistinct object. His hair, which is waved from the centre, falls in a long tress on his right shoulder. On his head he wears a crown. In treatment of details, this statuette resembles the Egyptian examples of 1st century A.C. where in Alexandria the cult of Harpocrates was very popular.

Toilet Articles

Toilet articles from Gandhara include ivory combs and hair pins, copper mirrors, antimony rods and phials, tooth picks, ear-cleaner, and flesh rubbers of which the copper mirrors and ivory combs are particularly interesting. The mirror is a circular disc provided with a handle of bone and ivory. The face of the mirror is smooth and slightly convex. The combs are made of ivory and bone. Their tops are curved and the teeth are sawn evenly and are slightly rounded at the ends. The majority of them are decorated with incised circlets or more elaborate designs like busts.

Inscriptions and Writing Materials

A number of Aramaic, Kharoshthi and Brahmi inscriptions were found at Taxila. A unique inscription in Aramaic was found in a wall at Sirkap. It mentions King Priya Darshi, his queen and sons and

Terracotta sealing representing the Buddha in explaining pose, Mirpurkhas

is datable to 3rd century B.C. The discovery of this stone record is of special interest since it confirms the view that Kharoshthi was derived at Taxila from Aramaic. Kharoshthi was the official script and inscriptions in Kharoshthi are found on cornice pieces, bracket figures or pedestals of the statues. Brahmi was also used at Taxila and birch bark pieces with Brahmi writing are available there. As regards the writing material, a number of copper, stone and pottery ink-pots, pens and writing tablets were found from Taxila sites and other regions of Gandhara.

Tools and Implements

Although no instruments of intricate type for making delicate jewellery are found, yet some tools of smith found in course of excavation at Taxila suggest a high standard of workmanship. The double headed hammers, anvils, clippers, chisels, axes and saws are good examples of the tools used by the craftsmen of Taxila. The agricultural implements are represented by spades, hoes, sickles, pick-axes and weeding-forks.

War Weapons

Though the chequered history of the Gandhara Valley is full of warfare, yet it is surprising to find a small number of war weapons. Whatever war weapons have been found they are neither large in number nor in their variety. They include swords, daggers, spears, javelins, arrows with iron head and

The Buddha in terracotta, Mirpurkhas

Stucco bust of Bodhisattva, Taxila Museum

Inscription on birch-bark, Taxila Museum

Punch marked silver coins, Indo-Greek and Kushan gold coins, Taxila Museum

bone arrow-heads, a helmet and a shield. An armour from Shaikhan Dheri is also worth recording. The swords are straight, double edged and pointed. A cross-guard is attached to the blade at the base of the hilt.

COINS

The history of coinage in Pakistan goes back to the 5th century B.C. The earliest coins of these series are silver bent bars with two punched symbols on one side following the Persian weight standard and double daric. The other type of indigenous coins generally known as punch-marked, have been recovered in thousands from almost all the ancient sites of the Gandhara region. These are thin circular or rectangular pieces with silver and copper alloy. These coins were in circulation in the north-western parts of West Pakistan during the 4th and 3rd centuries B.C. when the Mauryans were at the zenith of their power. A study of these coins reveals many interesting points. The symbols on these coins are as varied as numerous. The commonest of the symbols is the 'sun' which occurs on the obverse. Others of animals such as elephant, bull, rabbit and hunting dog also occur.

The earliest die-struck coins are seen after the invasion of Alexander the Great and they were popularised by the Bactrian Greek rulers of Gandhara in the second century B.C. The coins with a lion device were struck at Taxila and show not only a greater symmetry of shape but an advanced knowledge of die-cutting.

After the death of Ashoka in 232 B.C. Gandhara broke away from the Maurya empire. Soon the Bactrian Greeks conquered this region and established their rule which lasted for about one hundred years. The coinage of Bactrian Greeks provides yet another point of interest. Since their discovery more than thirty names of Greek and twenty nine Scythian and Parthian kings have been identified from the coin legends. Similarly, for the history of the Scythians and the Parthians, these coins are the only source of information. The names of the later Kushan kings too were first discovered from their coins. The coins from Gandhara, thus, have helped in reconstructing the early history of Pakistan.

The coins of Bactrian kings are executed in Greek style. The most important kings, judging from the large number of their coin types, were Demetrius (c. 190-150 B.C.), Menandar (160-140 B.C.), Strato I (156-140 B.C.) and Antialkidas (145 B.C.). They ruled over eastern and western Punjab and Gandhara.

In about 90 B.C. the Scythians overthrew the Bactrian Greeks. They conquered the Punjab and Taxila and extended their territory to the areas across the Indus to Gandhara. The most important rulers of the Scythians were Maues, Azes I (c. 38 B.C.), Azilizes and Azes II (c. 5 A.C.). During the rule of Azes II silver coins were replaced by billon and there was a corresponding deterioration in the design and execution of the coins.

By 19 A.C. the power of the Scythians disintegrated at the hands of the Parthians under Gondopharnes and during the 1st century A.C., their empire comprised the whole of West Pakistan, Seistan and southern Afghanistan.

In about the middle of the 1st century A.C. the Kushans conquered the territories of the present-day West Pakistan. The Kushan emperors for the first time established gold standard in place of silver and their gold coins became popular for international trade. After the experiment of the first Kushan Emperor, Kadphises I, who issued copper coins including a type bearing the king's head in imitation of the Roman Emperor Augustus, the second Kadphises fixed the gold standard. However, the most celebrated was Kanishka whose outstanding fame is due to his patronage of Buddhism. His coins are distinct in many respects from those of early Kushan Emperors. On the reverse of his gold and copper coins are portrayed both the Buddhist and non-Buddhist figures like Buddha, the Greek gods Helios, Herakles, Selene; the Hindu god Shiva and the Iranian gods Athsho, Oado and Nana. A standing figure of the king appears on the obverse. His successor Huvishka

Siddhartha on a ram-drawn chariot, Swat Museum

Terracotta bearded head of an ascetic, Taxila Museum

Stucco head of the Buddha, Taxila Museum

Stucco head of the Buddha, Taxila Museum

Earthenware pots, Taxila Museum

Stucco head of an Atlant, Taxila Museum

issued coins in abundance. His gold coin does not bear the full standing figure; it is either half length or merely the head. On one coin he is seated cross-legged while on another he is riding an elephant. His copper coins are more varied. Vasudeva of the same dynasty closely imitated Kanishka's standing figure type on gold coins.

In 3rd century A.C. the Great Kushana rule was brought to a close by the Sassanian invasion. Under their sovereignty a Kushana dynasty continued to rule and issue coins. But the Sassanian silver type became more common and survived the invasion of the Huns. Even during the 7th, 8th and 9th centuries, the coinage was a crude imitation of the Sassanian coins. About the end of the 9th century there grew up several petty kingdoms. Among these the Hindu Shahis of Gandhara issued a type of coin commonly known as the "Bull and Horseman" type which was later copied by the early Sultans of Delhi up to the reign of Ghias-ud-Din Balban.

JEWELLERY

A very fine and delicate collection of jewellery comes from Taxila. During the Mauryan period, the craftsmen had acquired great proficiency in the jeweller's art. They excelled especially in making delicate granular and filigree designs. The treatment of form was also important to them. A claw or tooth amulet is an excellent example of their workmanship. The

Toilet tray in grey schist showing a sea-monster and a half draped female figure, Taxila Museum

core of this amulet is of lead and is covered, except at the point, with a thin sheath of gold. On the front side, gold is decorated with a granulated design of small hexagons enclosed in beaded borders. The tooth of claw is pierced transversely by three holes for suspension. Yet another example of the Mauryan period, in beaded filigree, is an ear-ring of cylindrical form with five vertical beadings on the outside and five projecting knobs at the top.

Among the types of jewellery of the 1st century A.C. are the ear-pendants of various shapes, necklaces, girdles, breast-chains and belts, amulets and pendants, bangles and bracelets, torques, anklets and finger rings. The later specimens show marked western influence. A gold necklace, an ear-pendant of crescent type and a finger ring are the outstanding examples. The gold necklace consists of thirteen pendants and a terminal. The pendants are of two designs. One pendant consists of a small circle of gold centred, alternately, with a rock crystal and cornelian, and edged round with a double granulated beading. At the base is an open work obcordate attachment enclosing a triple cluster of granules and above it a spherical bead covered with fine granulation and pierced laterally for a string. The other design is of a quatrefoil form made up of six cloisons, the ob-

Toilet tray in grey schist showing a reclining lady with female attendants, Taxila Museum

cordate attachment below encloses triple clusters of granules. There are small spacing beads on the upper string. The terminal, which is composed of eight cloison, is inlaid with lapis-lazuli.

The ear-pendant consists of a plain leech crescent with clasp and a "bud" pendant suspended from it by a movable ring. The leech is of a thin gold-plate, shaped on core of pitch. The clasp which is attached by means of a ring hinge, is of double leech pattern ornamented at the centre with a female bust superimposed on a lotus rosette at the top of which is cinquefoil lotus with obcordate petals and at the bottom with a beaded circlet. The pendant ring is relieved on the outside with three rows of beads and granules and there are four small stars, besides the granulation, on the shoulder of the buds. At the top of the leech-crescent is a small ring, by which the ornament was suspended from the ear.

The finger ring is highly elaborate. The hoop is composed of an open work vine scroll between fine reel borders. In the scroll are trefoil cloisons, once enriched with stones or paste. The bezel which is pyramidal in shape comprises three oval box-setting diminishing in size towards the top.

MISCELLANEOUS OBJECTS

There are a number of objects which also deserve a mention. A small lion handle, glass tiles and bottles are a few examples out of an array of such materials.

Aramaic inscription on stone, Taxila Museum

Kharoshthi inscription on silver scroll, Taxila Museum

128

Hindu Period

NONE of the remains of Hindu temples in West Pakistan is likely to be earlier than the Arab conquest of Sind in 711 A.C. They fall into two groups, namely, the northern and the southern. The first group, belonging to the 8th to 10th centuries A.C. is situated amongst the barren hills of the Salt Range. The other belongs to the 12th to 14th centuries A.C. and lies near the southern border of Sind.

The northern group may again be divided into two sub-groups; (a) the eastern with Kashmiri affinities, aligned on the river Jhelum, which links Kashmir with the Indus basin, (b) the western, or more nor-mal Hindu type, aligned on the Indus. The eastern sub-group lies mostly in the Jhelum district and its best known example is the Malot temple, probably the site of Hiuen Tsang's Singhapura, ancient capital of the Salt Range. The temple is typical of the four-square Kashmiri style, with an elaborate recessed bay in each face flanked by fluted columns and capped by a trefoil arch. The roof was undoubtedly of stone, pyramidal in shape and stepped outwards in two or more stages. The columns are derived from a western style of architecture through Buddhist channels. The trefoiled arches derived from Buddhist buildings in which the trefoil represented the gable of an assembly

Terracotta head of an ascetic, Taxila Museum

Stucco head of Bodhisattva, Taxila Museum

Terracotta plaque depicting a female dancer and musicians, Lahore Fort, Department of Archaeology, Pakistan

hall or chaitya with side-aisles. The pyramidal roof is a copy of timber prototypes designed to resist the heavy snowfall of Kashmir. Thus the whole design is an original and striking rearrangement of Buddhist elements grafted upon a Himalayan timber-tradition.

The western sub-group of temples can be repre-

Toilet tray in green schist, Swat Museum

sented by the Kallar temple in Attock district and one of the temples of the southern Kafir Kot at Bilot in Dera Ismail Khan district. Both of these rise in the form of the convex-sided tower or shikhara, with a slightly projecting panelled bay in each side and both are elaborately fretted with patterns based remotely on the chaitya gable. Both also incorporate pilasters having vase-capitals with pendant foliage in a fashion first elaborated by the fifth and sixth century Gupta architects of the northern plain. And the link with the brick work of the stoneless plains is emphasised by the fact that the Kallar temple, although in the vicinity of good sandstone, is actually built with brick while the Kafir Kot temples produce a similar effect with close fitting blocks of soft, easily cut Kanjur stone, bound with mortar and formerly faced with plaster.

The southern Kafir Kot or Bilot series, together with a comparable group in the northern Kafir Kot, 24 miles away, deserves further comment. All, except one, of these temples are contained within the two fortifications. There are at least nine on the southern side and five on the northern. The individual temples differ in detail and to some extent in date also.

The interior of each shrine is formed by a square cella. By a succession of overlapping courses in the corners, the square is at varying heights reduced to an octagon from which springs a hemispherical dome constructed in horizontal courses. The larger shrines invariably have a high vaulted porch in front of the cella entrance. Above the cella there always rises a high and richly ornamented roof of the shikhara shape,

Bodhisattva head, Swat Museum

representing a truncated cone with gracefully curving angles. In the case of two other temples of the group with each other as pendants, the roof contains a second storey with smaller square cella approached by a staircase. The passage surrounding this second cella leads to another flight of stairs which give access to a third small chamber in the cupola. In other shrines such upper storeys are absent with a corresponding reduction in the height of the roof.

The outer side-walls of the shrines invariably show pilastered projections with a niche in the centre probably intended for the reception of an image. False niches of smaller dimensions usually decorate the flanking portions of each facade. Apart from the ever present pilasters and cinquefoil arches above the true niches, the decoration of the side walls varies greatly in richness. The roof is always the most ornate portion of the structure, being covered throughout with an intricate diaper of carving in which a "horseshoe" or "bee-hive" ornament plays the chief part.

In the larger temples, massive wooden beams were inserted diagonally across the corners of the cella-walls where these bear the circular drum of the dome. This incipient use of voussoir-construction, combined with the employment of mortar throughout the masonry may be interpreted either as evidence of an early post-Islamic date or a pre-Islamic infiltration of Iranian methods through the adjacent passes from the Iranian plateau. An eighth to tenth century date

Stone Relic Caskets, Taxila Museum

for these temples seems likely. No cult-object remain on the surface but there can be no doubt that these temples, in spite of the Buddhist influence, were Brahmanical.

The southern group of temples is concentrated in the district of Thar-Parkar. The best surviving member of this group of temples is the Jaina temple at Gori, about 14 miles north west of Virawah. It is built of local stone, with pillars and details of marble from Rajputana and consists of three parts, namely, an outer pavilion with marble pillars and a corbelled dome, leading to an inner pavilion of similar design but supplemented by small cella and the shrine itself, which formerly had a spire of typical Kathiawar pattern, adorned with rows of miniature spires. The domes, though not uncommon in Brahmanical and particularly Jaina temples and built on the Hindu corbel-system, probably owe their emphasis to Muslim influence.

Bust of the Buddha in stucco, Taxila Museum

Stucco head, Taxila Museum

Stucco head of the Buddha, Swat Museum

Stucco male head, Taxila Museum

Copper water pot, Taxila Museum

Stone bottle, Taxila Museum

Terracotta circular stamp, Taxila Museum

Copper utensils, Taxila Museum

SCULPTURE

Hindu period sculptures are scarce in West Pakistan. Paucity of such iconographic material has made it difficult to study the growth, development and its extension throughout West Pakistan in its proper perspective. Whatever is available was mostly found in the course of excavation in different parts of the province.

One of the most important and interesting discoveries is that of the bronze free standing image of Brahma from Brahmanabad in the district of Sanghar. It was a chance discovery at the time of ploughing. This four-faced image of Brahma stands three feet two inches high. Three of its faces—those of the sides and back are smaller than the front one and the hair-style is most elaborate. The figure has two hands—the left hand may have held a mala or rosary, the fore-finger and the thumb being in the position of counting the beads, while the right hand is turned up with the palm towards the body in the position of holding a book, the Vedas. The object hanging over the left shoulder is perhaps intended for an antelope skin. This bare-bodied figure wears one garment from the waist to the ankles. The sacred thread hangs over the left shoulder and the half-closed eyes are reminiscent of some of the Buddha images from the Mirpur Khas stupa and the Gandhara school of art. It is very difficult with a solitary image like this to arrive at a definite estimate of its age. But from the style of execution it seems to belong to about the 6th century A.C.

Another interesting piece is a sculptured block of marble from a stone temple of Virawah in Nagar Parkar. It is 6 feet and 9 inches in length and 2 feet and 7 inches in breadth. It is a highly ornamented door-jamb of a Vaishnava temple of about the 11th

Stucco head of a devotee, Taxila Museum

or 12th centuries A.C. and is of similar workmanship to that of many of the old temples in the adjoining region of North Gujrat. It is divided into two parts, the upper part being again sub-divided into three overlapping terraces and the central position of each of the three terraces is occupied by a free-standing male figure, probably Vishnu, attended by two female figures on his right and left. The lower part is centrally occupied by a standing figure of Vishnu within a tapering temple and flanked on either side by three female attendants.

The marble frame in relief, from a Shiva temple of Nagar Pakar, is another fine specimen of plastic art. The frame which surrounds the image is most elaborately carved with male and female figures on all sides. The figures are depicted in a joyous mood playing the vina, flute or drum, or dancing as if in ecstasy. The niche for the main deity is in the centre but is now empty. It is flanked on either side by elephants with riders, all paying homage. In the lower part of the frame there are four bays, two on each side of the main temple representation. These bays are also carved in the shape of temples containing male and female figures. In one, a lady is shown sitting on a stool with

Stucco head of the Buddha, Taxila Museum

Stucco figure of an attendant, Taxila Museum

Terracotta ram's head, Swat Museum

Water jar and tumbler, Taxila Museum

a lotus in hand while in the other a male is depicted playing the flute. From the style of execution, this marble frame can be dated to the 10th or 11th centuries A.C.

Another door jamb in stone relief showing the goddess Gauri in a temple with some indistinct objects in her hands and attended by two club-bearing guards, is a very interesting example of lithic art from Thar-Parkar. It can be dated to about 10th century A.C.

Two stone images of Kuvera and Vishnu, from the Dharmarajika stupa area of Taxila, form very interesting finds of an earlier period. The figure of Kuvera, executed in the round, is standing with a long spear in the right hand while a parrot-like bird is sitting on his left hand. The figure is profusely bejewelled and wears a dress to the knee. A halo at its back and a tiara on its head is in the fashion of the Buddhist sculptures. The image is in conformity with the Gandhara style of execution and is dated to about 4th-5th century A.C.

The stone miniature Vishnu from Taxila is yet another very interesting specimen from the iconographical point of view. It is a free standing image with four hands. The upper right and left hands hold lotus and conch, while the lower right hand holds the

Plain pottery, Taxila Museum

Plain and perforated pottery, Swat Museum

Terracotta toys, Taxila Museum

Jars and a goblet, Taxila Museum

Gold ring, Taxila Museum

Gold bracelet, Taxila Museum

Gold ear pendant, Taxila, National Museum, Karachi

mace and the left holds the wheel. The drapery is up to the knee and shows the usual Gandhara folds. The sacred thread hangs on the left shoulder. Profusely bejewelled, it has a conical crest on its head in the Parthian style and has a halo at the back. In between the stretched legs, there is a representation of a human head. The image, executed in the round, is in the Gandhara style and is dated to the 8th century A.C.

Silver wares, Taxila Museum

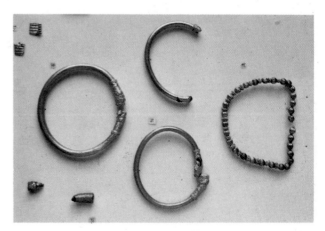

Gold bangles and a necklace, Taxila Museum

OTHER ART SPECIMENS

Besides the sculptural objects discussed above, a few specimens of other art objects also form valuable part of the cultural heritage of Pakistan. Pre-Muslim levels at Banbhore have yielded a variety of interesting objects which include terracotta figurines, both human and animal, fragments of stone sculpture and fine ceramic specimens. A moulded terracotta female head with well-developed features and dress is interesting. It stands out as a class by itself in superiority of technique and execution.

From the temple area of Banbhore, an ornamental pedestal with thick lime plaster and other architectural decorations were recovered. Near the pedestal, two votive Shiva lingams—one with yoni—were found lying on the floor. Similar monolithic Shiva lingams have been unearthed from other parts of the site. The Shiva cult appears to have been popular during the period immediately before the advent of the Muslims.

Other interesting finds include a large number of pottery moulds with geometric-cum-floral design and human or animal representations. One mould depicts a dancing couple in typical pre-Muslim style while another depicts a frieze with elephant and sun-flower. Mention must also be made of the Sassanian type of decorated pottery vessels with friezes in relief showing birds and animals within dotted circles.

Excavations in Lahore Fort have brought forth some interesting pre-Muslim objects of great art value. Among the human figurines, the female figure of a mother goddess with well-developed facial features and an elongated head-dress is interesting. Beaked-nose female figurines and a male figurine showing a conical head-dress in the Scythian style are fascinating. A number of animal figurines were also discovered, among them a saddled-horse type.

Stone bead necklace with pendant, Tulamba, Department of Archaeology, Pakistan

An amphora deserves particular mention. It is painted with intricate geometric and floral designs with black paint on a whitish background. Male and female figures, spotted cows, and peacocks in fighting mood are represented on the pot in a remarkably life-like manner. One standing female figure wears a long dress and holds a bunch of flowers in her hand. Another figure, perhaps a goddess, wears a crown-like head-dress and ear-stud of typical Hindu style. The male figure, standing in front of an elephant and holding a thunderbolt, perhaps represents Indra. The whole scene is mythical and the amphora was no doubt meant for ritual purposes. A votive tank resembling those recovered from the 2nd century A.C. levels at Taxila was also found. It was used by Hindu maidens for the rituals of Yamapukur-Brata. Terracotta plaques also form an interesting group from the pre-Muslim levels of Lahore Fort. Particular mention may be made of one depicting a bejewelled dancing girl flanked by two male figures playing on the drum. The scene is very life-like and reminds us of the famous bhangra dance of the Punjab.

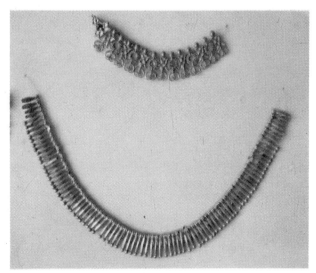

Gold necklaces, Taxila Museum

Stone bead necklaces, Swat Museum

Silver anklet, Taxila Museum

General view of excavations, Charsadda

Golden ear pendants, Taxila Museum

Temple E at Bilot Kafirkot, D.I. Khan

Temple D at Bilot Kafirkot, D.I. Khan

Temple C at Bilot Kafirkot, D. I. Khan

145

Temple A at Bilot Kafirkot, D. I. Khan

Brahma in brass, Brahmanabad, National Museum, Karachi

Marble door jamb, Gori temple, Tharparkar, National Museum, Karachi

Siva-lingam in situ, Banbhore

Bodhisattva Maitreya, Taxila, National Museum, Karachi.

A goddess (?) with a spear in hand, Swat Museum

Gori temple, Tharparkar

EAST PAKISTAN

Geography and History

EAST PAKISTAN with a vast, flat, riverain plain watered by the three great river system of the Ganges, Brahmaputra and Meghna and their innumerable tributaries and branches, has a unique charm of its own. Its annual rainfall is one of the highest in the world. The exotic growth and variety of its flora and fauna is a cardinal fact essential to an understanding of the land and its people. This feature has left its mark in every sphere of life and culture of this part of Pakistan.

Nature has divided East Pakistan into three distinct parts which fairly correspond with the major political divisions of ancient times. Varendra on the north was a sub-division of Pundravardhana-Bhukti; the great alluvial plain of the Ganges-Brahmaputra in the south bore the name of Bang or Vanga; while the eastern hilly area beyond the river Meghna formed the ancient land of Samatata.

Bang or Vanga is really the name of a people who

Main temple showing position of terracotta plaques, Paharpur

Ante-chamber of Main temple, Paharpur

inhabited this region in the remote past. But, by the time of the Hindu epics, the Ramayana and the Mahabharata, they had gained some political recognition and are mentioned in a list of peoples that entered into political relation with the Aryans of mid-India.

The name of Pundravardhana-Bhukti preserves the memory of the ancient inhabitants of the plateau called the Pundras. They were regarded by the Aryans with contempt and are described as a wild barbarian tribe or Dasyus in the Aitareya Brahmana.

As regards the pre-historic period of East Pakistan, nothing is precisely known save some megalithic stones found in the Sylhet, Chittagong and Comilla districts. The historic period of East Pakistan began in the 3rd century B.C. when Pundravardhana-Bhukti or North Bengal lay within the Mauryan empire of Ashoka. This fact is conclusively proved by the discovery of the Brahmi inscription from Mahasthangarh in the Bogra district. The celebrated Chinese pilgrim Hiuen Tsang visited Pundravardhana or Pan-na-fa-tan-na between the years 639 to 645 A.C. and noticed, besides other Buddhist institutions, a large stupa called Po-shi-po or Vasu Vihara which was erected by Ashoka on the body relic of the Buddha. The pilgrim also tells us that the Buddha stayed there for three months to preach his faith. All these references clearly bear testimony to the close association of the region with the Mauryan rule. Discovery of terracotta figurines of the Sunga period at Mahasthan and Kushan coins in several places of Bengal gives us just a peep into the period intervening between the Maurya and Gupta rule. A number of epigraphic records and copper plate inscriptions leaves no doubt that Bengal formed an integral part of the Gupta empire down to the end of the 6th century A.C. with the exception of Samatata which corresponds roughly with south-eastern Bengal including the present district of Comilla. The kingdom of Samatata although acknowledging the suzerainty of the Gupta emperors, retained absolute autonomy in internal administration.

Towards the close of the 6th century, the Gupta empire disintegrated and was succeeded by a chaotic struggle for power amongst a succession of petty rulers. This state of anarchy is metaphorically described by the Tibetan historian Taranath as that of fishes, the strong preying on the weak.

In order to put an end to anarchy, the people of Bengal elected Gopala as their ruler. The Pala dynasty formed by Gopala about the middle of the 8th century A.C. was one of the most remarkable among the ancient dynasties and its rule for nearly four centuries established, for the first time, a long and stable government in Bengal. From the evidence of copper plate grants and pillar inscriptions, we know not only the genealogy of the dynasty but also a great deal about the system of administration. The Palas exercised direct administrative control over Bengal and Bihar. Although the Palas were Buddhist, there is evidence that Hinduism also enjoyed a large measure of tolerance. It was during this period that many new Hindu temples were established in Bengal under royal patronage.

Besides the erection of several temples and viharas in different parts of their empire, the biggest and most important of these was established at Paharpur which received royal patronage from the early Pala rulers. Under their rule, there grew up a separate and independent school of art known as Pala art. According to Taranath, the Tibetan historian, during the reign of Dharmapala and Devapala, there flourished two great religious sculptors named Dhiman and Vitapala in Varendra, and it is believed that some of the fine specimens of medieval sculpture, found in Bengal are the work of these artists or of the schools established by them.

The glory and brilliance of the Pala empire declined after the death of Devapala in the middle of the 9th century A.C. but about the end of the 10th century A.C. its glory was revived under Mahipala I. Towards the middle of the 11th century A.C. the fortunes of the Palas again suffered a reverse and Bengal was over-run in turn by a series of foreign invasions from the east, west and the south. The Pala kingdom was shaken to its very foundation and gradually reduced to a minor power.

In the 12th century A.C., the Brahmanical Senas, replaced the Palas and Varendra became a part of their dominions. The Sena kings do not seem to have had any leaning towards Buddhism and it does not

Terracotta plaques at the basement of the Central Shrine, Mainamati

appear to have received any patronage from them and Buddhist institutions soon disappeared for want of royal support. It was from the Senas that Bengal was seized by the Muslims within less than a century.

When political turmoil was going on in Varendra in the 7th century A.C., the realm of Samatata was enjoying peace and prosperity under the rule of the Buddhist Khadga dynasty which ruled from the middle of the 7th century to the beginning of 8th century A.C. The seat of administration was at Jaykarmanta-vasaka which has been identified with the present village of Badkamta, about 12 miles west of Comilla town.

After the Khadgas, the Devas, a new Buddhist dynasty seem to have established its power in Samatata with the administrative centre round Mainamati hills. They appear to have been the contemporaries of the early Palas, the powerful rulers of North Bengal. How long their rule lasted or what relations they had with the Palas, is not precisely known at present. The next known rulers of Samatata are the celebrated Chandras, yet another Buddhist line of rulers, who came to power in the beginning of the 10th century A.C. and continued their uninterrupted rule for about 150 years up to the middle of the 11th century A.C.

Terracotta sealing, Mainamati Museum

Their seat of government was at Vikrampur near Dacca and their relation with the neighbours, particularly the Palas, was not a happy one and the Chandra rulers inflicted crushing defeats on the Palas of North Bengal. During their rule, Samatata enjoyed all round prosperity in the sphere of cultural, religious and political activities.

The Chandras were supplanted by the Vaishnavite Varmans, in the middle of the 11th century A.C. and this period is very obscure. But the evidences of Mainamati excavation indicate that the importance of this area as the nerve-centre of south-east Bengal remained undiminished till the advent of the Muslims in the beginning of the 13th century A.C.

Close view of central shrine showing position of terracotta plaques, Mainamati

The stupas at Kotila Mura, Mainamati

General view of central shrine, Mainamati

SALBAN VIHARA MONASTERY, MAINAMATI
GENERAL PLAN

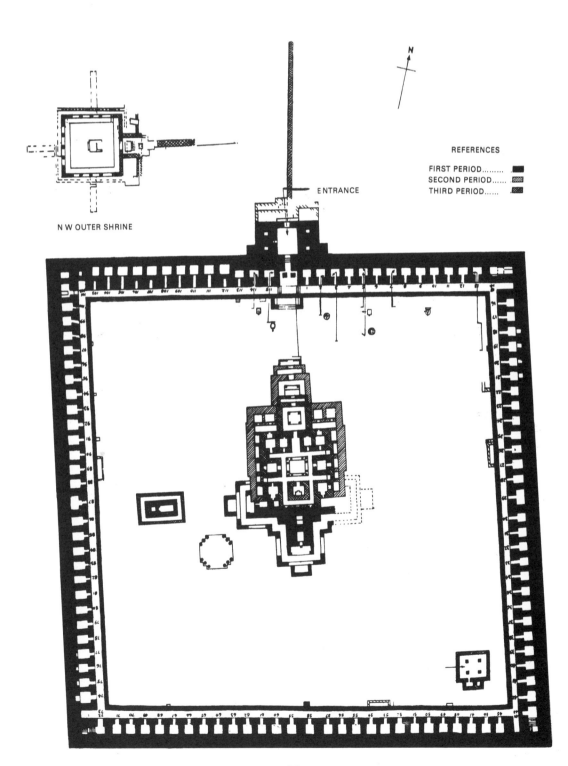

N W OUTER SHRINE

ENTRANCE

REFERENCES

FIRST PERIOD.........
SECOND PERIOD......
THIRD PERIOD......

Buddhist Period

MONASTERY AND STUPA ARCHITECTURE

EAST PAKISTAN is the last stronghold of Buddhism in the sub-continent. It appears from certain Vinaya Texts that Buddhism was introduced here even before the rule of Ashoka in the 3rd century B.C. During Ashoka's time, however, the religion received fresh impetus, especially in view of its closer proximity to the region of the Master's birth place. The flourishing period of Buddhism in Bengal is best reflected in the records of a number of Chinese pilgrims who came here between the 6th and 8th century A.C. and is also confirmed by a number of royal copper plate grants discovered in different parts of Bengal.

Buddhism received royal patronage in East Pakistan, between the 7th and 13th centuries A.C., from such important ruling dynasties as the Khadgas, the Devas, the Palas, the Chandras and the minor ruling chiefs of Pattikera who ruled between the 11th-13th centuries A.C. During the rule of these dynasties, many shrines and monasteries grew up in different parts of Bengal, the remains of which are coming to

EXCAVATIONS AT PAHARPUR
DISTRICT RAJSHAHI
GENERAL PLAN

SCALE OF FEET

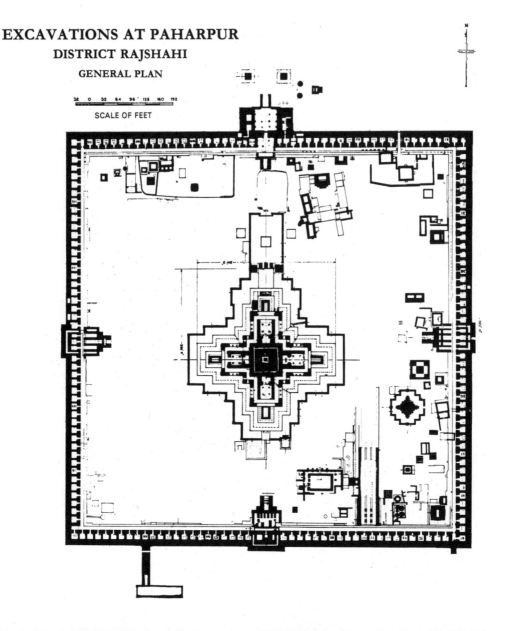

Monastic cells, Mainamati

Terracotta plaques in position, Mainamati

light as a result of excavation. Buddhist remains of the Pala period, mostly lie in Varendra or north Bengal while the rest are in Samatata or south-east Bengal. As a result of excavation, Buddhist remains of architectural and historical significance have been unearthed at Mahasthangarh in Bogra, Paharpur in Rajshahi, and Mainamati in Comilla district.

Mahasthangarh

The Mahasthangarh site in the Bogra district, re-

presents the earliest known city site in East Pakistan. Archaeological evidence testified to its existence as far back as the 3rd century B.C. and it continued to flourish till the 15th-16th centuries A.C. It was the provincial headquarters successively of the Mauryans, the Guptas, the Palas and other minor Hindu dynasties. The extensive fortified city on the western bank of the river Karatoya, represents, therefore, about eighteen hundred years of intensive occupation.

Innumerable mounds bearing local names are lying

Detail view of terracotta plaques, Paharpur

Sanctum in the Central Shrine, Mainamati

Interior view of a monastic cell, Mainamati

General view of excavations at the northern fortification wall, Mahasthangarh

scattered in and around the citadel mound. Sporadic excavation of the site in pre-Independence days and systematic operations by the Department of Archaeology in recent years, have brought to light important structural and other antiquarian remains which, to a large extent, help reconstruct the historical past of East Pakistan.

Excavations at Bairagi Bhita mound exposed the remains of two large but fragmentary Buddhist temples of the early and late Pala period. The early Pala temple measures 98 ft. in length and 42 ft. in width. Two highly ornamental pillars, square in section with chamfered corners, were found in the course of excavation.

At a short distance, to the south of the former temple, another temple of about the 11th century A.C. was unearthed. This temple measures 111 ft. from east to west and 57 ft. from north to south and was provided with a porch and a brick paved platform around it.

Excavation of the northern rampart of the citadel of Mahasthangarh revealed four principal rebuilding phases, the latest of which belongs to the Muslim

Terracotta head, Mahasthangarh Museum

period of 15th-16th centuries A.C. and the earliest to the Gupta period. The two intervening periods are assigned to the Pala and pre-Islamic. The earliest Gupta period was represented by two massive parallel walls running towards the Govinda Bhita temple in the north.

The most imposing building complex excavated at Mahasthan is the Govinda Bhita, on the double bend of the Karatoya, a ruin outside the northern rampart wall of the city.

It represents four building periods, commencing from the late Gupta period to the Muslim occupation. The earlier building phase on the west, dated to the 6th-7th centuries A.C., is represented by a massive wall with 16 off-sets. It bears affinity with the basement wall of the main temple at Paharpur.

Another interesting type of early temple architecture in Bengal can be studied in the exposed ruins of Gokul near Mahasthangarh. The gigantic Medh mound at Gokul when excavated still retained an imposing height of 43 ft. and presented the appearance of a honey-comb of innumerable blind cells, arranged indiscriminately around a central circular shrine.

A closer study, however, clearly indicates that this apparently meaningless cellular construction served the purpose of providing a solid foundation for a lofty superstructure. In plan, it is a polygon of twenty-

Bodhisattva Padmapani in bronze, Mainamati Museum

four sides with a circular central structure, which contained a gold leaf bearing the figure of a bull in repousse relief. The main shrine, a lofty structure, was placed on a high podium of a solid foundation raised by means of four massive walls forming a quadrangular platform. The intervening spaces were made compact by erecting a cross wall and filling up the cellular enclosure with earth. Subsidiary smaller quadrangles were added on four sides to lend further strength to the high and solid foundation, and these in turn were revetted outside by additional rows of walls and cells.

This buttressed quadrangle not only ensured stability to the whole building but also added grandeur and an imposing character to the temple which stood on it. No evidence is left to ascertain the actual form and appearance of the superstructure. It is, however, reasonable to assume, from the different levels of the successive quadrangles, that the whole edifice rose in a tapering mass with graded terraces and capped by the usual finials. The Medh mound of Gokul can be

Bodhisattva in bronze, Mainamati Museum

assigned to the 6th century A.C.

Paharpur

The Buddhist shrine and monastery, at Paharpur in the district of Rajshahi, are the largest known Buddhist ruins south of the Himalayas. The central shrine is so high that it is locally known as "Pahar" or hill.

Buddhism secured a strong grasp in East Pakistan from the time of the Palas who patronized it by establishing numerous shrines and monasteries in different parts of their kingdom. The best example of their patronage is witnessed at Paharpur where Dharamapala established the famous Somapura Vihara in 800 A.C.

The monastery of Paharpur is about 920 ft. square externally with 177 cells for the monk-students. Each cell, about 13 ft. long, opens on to a great court through verandas. The monastery is approached through a monumental northern gateway, with a pillared forehall. Among other buildings, the most notable are a long hall, probably the refectory, near the south eastern corner and a lavatory outside the

Hara-Gauri in bronze, Paharpur

163

Lion, terracotta plaque, Mainamati Museum   *Lotus, terracotta plaque, Mainamati Museum*

monastery. The latter was approached by a raised bridge from the southern enclosure wall across an archway.

The most striking feature in the monastery is that as many as 92 cells contain ornamental pedestals. The cells were used to accommodate the monks, attached to the vihara. The pedestals in the cells were for ceremonial purpose.

The stupendous establishment with the surrounding 177 cells, a gateway, votive stupas, minor chapels, a tank and numerous other structures for the convenience of the inmates is dominated by the great central shrine, conspicuous by its lofty height of 70 ft. It is remarkable for its architectural design and splendour. It is pyramidal in elevation and cruciform in plan with angles of projection between the arms. It is raised in three terraces, each with a circumbulatory passage, and fenced off by a parapet wall. The lower terrace is approached by a grand staircase from the north. This style of architecture with a complicated scheme of decoration of walls with carved brick cornices and friezes of terracotta plaques, developed in East Pakistan during the Pala period. Later on it profoundly influenced the architectural efforts of south-east Asia, especially Burma and Java.

The scheme of embellishment of the basement walls of the main shrine is unique and artistic. The monotony of the plain surface of the walls is broken by the insertion of stone bas-relief at angles of the projections and at intervals in specially built recesses in the middle of the wall of the first terrace. The interme-

diate niches contain 63 sculptures of Brahmanical deities of the late Gupta epoch. The outer face of the walls of the upper terraces have been decorated by projecting cornices of ornamented bricks and bands of terracotta plaques, set in recessed panels, which run in a single row round the basement and in double rows around the circumambulatory passage in the upper terraces.

Mainamati

The Lalmai-Mainamati ridge of Comilla district is dotted with numerous Buddhist remains of which three sites—those of Salban Vihara, Kotila Mura and Charpatra Mura, have been excavated. Salban Vihara, the major site, is situated in the middle of the ridge at a distance of about six miles west of Comilla town.

As a result of excavation at Salban Vihara, remains of a central shrine and a large Buddhist monastery have come to light. Built roughly on a square plan, the monastery is a monumental edifice with sides 550 feet long, containing a total of 115 cells, arranged round the central shrine. It is in a good state of preservation and its general character is one of solidity and massiveness. The cells are connected by a veranda which runs in front of the cells. With its massive enclosure walls, the monastery of Salban Vihara is provided with only one elaborate gateway complex flanked by guard-rooms on the north.

The monastic cells are all 12 ft. square. These were provided with a threshold, a wooden door and corbelled niches in the side walls. The niches were used for the reception of votive images, oil lamps and miscellaneous material.

A large pillared hall with two attached chambers, in the south-eastern corner of the courtyard appears to have been the community dining hall of the monastery. The courtyard is clustered with a number of subsidiary shrines.

Constructed of burnt brick, the central shrine of Salban Vihara is an imposing monument. It is ringed by an embellished plinth with pointed angles and recessed corners and resembles, in plan, a cross with chapels built in the projecting arms facing the cardinal points. The basement walls of both the eastern and western projections are in a perfect state of preservation. They are decorated with two courses of ornamental bricks and a band of sculptured terracotta plaques, illustrating in base-relief the mythology and folk-lore of the country. The shrine measures 170 ft. arm to arm. From its size, it appears that the structure attained a considerable height. The approach to the shrines was from the north, through a stepped terrace.

The architectural details, the specimens of sculptural art as well as other objects discovered at this site, tend to prove it to be contemporary with the large monastic establishment of Paharpur in the Rajshahi district. The square layout of the monastery, the cruciform plan of the central shrine and the terracotta plaques found at both the sites are very similar. The monastic establishment of Salban Vihara was built by King Bhavadeva, the fourth ruler of the Buddhist ruling dynasty of the Devas of Samatata, as is evidenced by the discovery of clay seals.

In spite of being considerably damaged, the shrine presents a fully developed and finished example of indigenous Buddhist architecture in Bengal of the 7th and 8th centuries evolved as a result of the synthesis of Hindu-Buddhist elements in the last phase of Buddhism.

Kotila Mura Stupas

Excavations at Kotila Mura, two miles north of Salban Vihara, have revealed three stupas, representing the three jewels of Buddhism, i.e., Buddha, Dharma and Sangha, built in the traditional style. These stupas have a square ornamental plinth on which rests the circular drum and the hemispherical dome. The stupas were built on the traditional style of Buddhist architecture as is evidenced from the shape of bronze stupa discovered from excavations. The central stupa contains eight box-chambers, in the form of a Dharma-Chakra. The superstructures of the other two are of solid brick masonry. Undoubtedly, this group of stupas is unique in character and is the first of its kind so far discovered in East Pakistan.

Avalokisteshvara in stone, Mainamati Museum

SCULPTURE

In East Pakistan, stone sculptures of the Buddhist pantheon belong to the Pala school, ranging in date from 750 A.C. to 1250 A.C. Earlier sculptures were mostly in perishable materials such as wood or clay, but later, stone was introduced. They are mainly carved in an exceptionally fine grained black-basalt, quarried from the Rajmahal hills. The masterly hand of the artists gave a highly lustrous and glossy surface to the material depicting minute details of ornamentation with a graceful softness which becomes almost sensual. Another durable material, though less frequently used for making images, was bronze or octo-alloy which was sometimes found gold-plated. These metal images testify to the high state of excellence which the art of casting metals had attained in this region.

The art trends of the period from the 8th to the 13th centuries A.C. in terracotta, stone and wood, are marked by a visible change which developed distinct-

Tara, terracotta plaque, Paharpur Museum

ive elements highly imbued with the folk art of East Pakistan. Their chief characteristics are richly bedecked figures with stiff bodies on a background of carved stalae. However, the development of bronze images produced under the skill of master artists like Dhiman and Bitapal, are indeed noteworthy. Together with these, the art of wood carving also attained a high standard of proficiency.

Buddhism spread in East Pakistan during the rule of the later Guptas, the Khadgas, the Palas, the Devas and the Chandras. Among these rulers, the Palas of North Bengal, the Chandras and the Devas of Samatata were ardent Buddhists and under their patronage there grew up many well-organized monasteries and stupas as at Paharpur and Mainamati. But, by the end of the 8th century A.C. Buddhism lost much of its simplicity and it developed into a new phase of the Tantric cult which, indeed, had a greater appeal to the masses. This cult, with numerous schisms, brought Buddhism nearer to Hinduism so much so that most of the deities became objects of worship common both to Buddhists and to Hindus.

However, it is evident that during this period of art development in East Pakistan, simple Mahayana and Hinayana sects of Buddhism developed new

Terracotta plaque depicting dancing girls and a piper, Dacca Museum

trends. The primary deities of the Mahayana pantheon are the Adi Buddha and the Adi Prajna, who may very aptly be compared with the Universal Father and Universal Mother in the hierarchy of gods. Five Dhyani Buddhas, deep in eternal meditation, who emanated from the pair, are Vairochana, Akshobhya, Ratna-Sambhava, Amitabha and Amoghasiddhi, to which sometimes a sixth Buddha called Vajrasattva is added. These Buddhas are positive and, for the purpose of creation, each of them has an active counter-part called the Bodhisattva who, in successive ages, uphold the creation and then merge again into their original source. The most common among the Bodhisattvas are Avalokiteshvara, Manjushri and Maitreya.

The Bodhisattvas have, in their turn, a female Shakti, the most famous of them being Tara. Taras of different aspects such a Prajnaparamita, Marichi, Parnashavari, Chunda, Hariti etc., are abundant in East Pakistan. Among the more important varieties of Taras emanating from different Dhyani Buddhas, we may mention Khadiravani-Tara, Vajra-Tara and Bhrikuti-Tara. Khadiravani-Tara, popularly known as Shyama-Tara on account of her green colour is the most common of such images seen in East Pakistan. She holds a blue lotus in her hand and is generally accompanied by Ashoka-kanta and Ekajata, her two companions.

Below this group, divinities are taken from the popular worship of Bengal such as Jambhala, Hevajra, Heruka, Mahamaya and Kalachakra. The next group consists of the Dharmapalas or the "Defenders of the Faith" such as Kuvera, Yama, Hayagriva, Mahakala etc. The last group represents the divine personages of whom the sixteen Mahasthaviras, Nagarjuna and Padmasambhava are noteworthy.

The earliest known Buddhist image in East Pakistan is from Biharail in Rajshahi district. It is datable to early in the 6th century A.C. This standing image, carved on Chunar sandstone, shows delicacy in limbs, roundness of form, refined expression and diaphanous dress—all indicating an affinity with the classical style of Gupta art.

Two stone sculptures, discovered from the deep shaft of the central stupa of Kotila Mura at Mainamati, represent a unique group of sculptures, differing from all the known schools of sculptural art of the sub-continent. They include two large panels in grey coloured shale, both in stalae. The central figures of these panels are the Buddha and the Bodhisattva respectively, seated on the lotus throne. In one of them, the pose of the central figure, a four-armed Bodhisattva Avalokiteshvara, is highly interesting. He is accompanied by a multitude of smaller figures

Padmapani, terracotta plaque, Mainamati Museum

of Buddha, Bodhisattva and other Buddhist deities, all placed on lotus seats and joined together by long lotus stalks and attended by lay worshippers at the bottom. In the other panels also, the Buddha in Dharmachakra Mudra is attended on all sides by Buddhist gods and goddesses. All the elements in the composition of the panels are well-knit to form a picture of exceptional beauty. From the style of execution, these panels can be dated not later than the 7th century A.C.

Among the subsidiary deities, we should also mention Jambhala, usually associated with Buddha Ratna-Sabhava and Heruka, an emanation of Akoshbhya. Jambhala is the Buddhist god of riches and king of Yakshas. He is represented as a pot-bellied figure with squat dwarfish features. The Jambhala figures found in East Pakistan show all these characteristics and are invariably depicted as pressing with their left hands the neck of a mongoose vomitting jewels. One such typical representation of Jambhala is a miniature made of local stone, found during excavations at Mainamati. It is a very fine specimen with all the iconographic details and is now displayed in the Mainamati museum.

Two unique stone images of Heruka—one in the

Detail view of terracotta plaques, Paharpur

Dacca museum and the other in the Mainamati museum—are remarkable. The former is from Badkamta (Comilla) and the latter from Kachua (Comilla) and they are among the rarest finds in East Pakistan. Vigorously carved on stalae with flames issuing out of their borders, the figures are shown dancing in an ecstatic pose—the Dacca museum specimen is on a lotus while that of the Mainamati Museum is on a corpse. Both are decorated with long garland of skulls and other ornaments. Two hands of the Dacca Museum piece are broken while only the right hand of the Mainamati Museum is broken. The Mainamati specimen holds a skull in his left hand. There is a long Khatvanga (a type of club) placed along its left shoulder and both bear an effigy of Akshobhya among the flaming hair. These Tantric Buddhist icons can be dated to the 11th century A.C. Another deity, Hevajra, in Yab-yum attitude with its Shakti was found at Paharpur. It has eight heads and sixteen arms which hold skull cups.

Taras of different varieties are available in the museums of Dacca, Rajshahi and Mainamati. Among them the Khadiravani Tara, Vajra Tara, Bhirkuti Tara and Shyama Tara are prominent. They mostly range in date from the 10th to the 12th centuries A.C. Other common Buddhist deities from East Pakistan are Chunda, Parnashavari, Shitatapatra, now being displayed in various museums of the Province.

Excavations at Mainamati have yielded hundreds of bronze statues of Buddha, Bodhisattva, Tara, Manjushri, Sarvani and numerous other Buddhist deities. They reveal iconographic developments reflecting changes in the character of Buddhism from the Mahayana type to Tantric form during the 7th-8th centuries A.C.

These images can be divided into two groups—crudely executed specimens showing the effects of mass production and the other, a large and comparatively superior group, which is characterised by a great refinement of art and precision of execution. This latter group seems to have been influenced by the Pala School of Art.

The statues of the Buddha show gracefulness and divine expression in the face. In most of the images, the right hand is shown touching the earth while the left one is placed on the lap. Buddha images in a meditative pose also occur. Bodhisattvas are all profusely bejewelled and are seated on the lotus throne holding a lotus stalk in left hand.

Images of Tara and other female deities, seated on the lotus throne, are also highly ornamented. Sometimes they are multiple-handed and exhibit the boon-bestowing pose in the right hand. The image of Sarvani is somewhat larger and is shown standing on a lion.

COINS

The importance of coins as datable evidence for fixing chronology is indeed very great. In East Pakistan these are very scarce, particularly in the Buddhist period. The earliest coins of the 1st-2nd centuries B.C. the punch marked type, come from the Mahasthangarh excavations. These coins depict various symbols, such as the Swastika, wheel, cross, deer, elephant, bull and a plant design. Excavations at Mainamati have yielded a considerable number of gold and silver coins of the Gupta and Deva rulers.

The Mainamati silver coins in three denominations show a humped couchant bull on the obverse with the legends of Pattikera, Dharma-Vijaya or Lalitakara. The Triratna symbol, surmounted by sun and the moon symbols, occur on the reverse. The discovery of these coins at Mainamati is of great significance. Their number, association, find-spot and other available evidence strengthens the view that these coins were issued locally by a well-established and prosperous dynasty of independent Deva rulers. On palaeographical grounds, these coins are assignable to 7th-8th centuries A.C., the date assigned to the Devas.

Buddha surrounded by other deities in bronze,
Mainamati Museum

Gold and silver coins, Mainamati Museum

One of the gold coins from Mainamati is of special interest. It is an imitation of the Gupta "Lakshmi and Archer" type and is inscribed with the same legend Bhangala Mrigankasya as found on the seals of the copper plate grants of the Deva kings discovered at Mainamati. Thus they seem to have been issued by one of the Deva rulers. If the assumption is correct, it is an emphatic indication of the economic stability and prosperity of the Devas.

MINOR ARTS

Minor art objects also form important finds in the Buddhist period of East Pakistan. Two relic caskets, both of bronze, come from Mainamati. The smaller one, measuring 5.3 inches in height, is a fine specimen. Originally fitted with a bronze stopper, it has a serrated rim and a ridge on its shoulder. The larger one is of squat globular shape, fitted with a knobbed lid. No relic was found inside any of them.

Hundreds of unbaked clay votive stupas encasing bone relics and tiny clay inscribed sealings were found at Mainamati and Paharpur. These miniature stupas were prepared in a mould portraying the cylindrical drum, square harmika and the finial. Besides, a large number of terracotta sealings of different sizes depicting the Buddhist creed are also important art objects from Mainamati, Paharpur and Mahasthangarh. Among them, two sealings—one each from Mainamati, and Paharpur—deserve particular mention, for they contain inscription of historic importance. Their upper part depicts the royal emblems of the Devas and the Palas represented by a Dharma-

Chakra flanked by two deer and in the lower there are three lines of inscriptions. The Mainamati sealing reads "Shri Bhavadeva, the builder of the great monastic establishment for the venerable monks" while that of Paharpur reads "Dharmapala, the builder of the great monastery of Somapura for the venerable monks."

Buddhist period metal objects from East Pakistan include gold, silver and bronze ornaments, such as finger rings, ear-rings, bangles, circular silver ingots, iron nails and hinges. Various types of precious and semi-precious stone beads are common. Terracotta objects include animal figurines, toys and beads. Glass and shell objects consist mostly of bangles. Ornamental bricks with different patterns were recovered in large numbers from Paharpur, Mainamati and Mahasthangarh.

Mainamati Copper Plates

The inscribed Copper Plates discovered from Mainamati excavations are the most important historic documents which have furnished information of great significance. They are royal grants of different ruling dynasties of south-east Bengal. Among the copper plate finds two of them belong to the Devas, a new dynasty of Buddhist rulers hitherto unknown in the history of Bengal. The seals of these copper

Terracotta Sunga plaque, Mahasthangarh Museum

171

Terracotta sealing, Mahasthangarh Museum

The Buddha in black stone, Dinajpur, Rajshahi Museum

plates contain the royal insignia of Buddhist Dharma-chakra flanked by two seated deer, and below this symbol runs the royal title of the Deva rulers. One of the copper plates was issued by Ananda Deva and endorsed by his son and successor Bhava Deva. Its genealogy portion mentions the names of two more earlier Deva rulers—Shanti Deva and Vira Deva, respectively the grand father and father of the issuing ruler Ananda Deva. They were Buddhists as evidenced by their imperial titles. From the style of writing of copper plates, the Devas seem to have ruled during the 7th-8th centuries A.C.

Three out of four copper plates, discovered from the excavated site of Charpatra Mura at Mainamati, belong to the well-known Buddhist royal family of the Chandras of south-east Bengal. They are known to have ruled there during the 10th and 11th centuries A.C. But before the discovery of these inscriptions their history and genealogy was incomplete. The present copper plates furnish for the first time their correct and complete genealogy along with their military exploits and social, political and religious conditions of the contemporary period. The royal emblem of the Chandras, as found on the copper royal grants, is similar to that of the Devas, but instead of the royal title as seen in the royal seal of the Devas, here we find the name of the grant issuing rulers. Among the three Chandra copper plates two were issued by Ladaha Chandra while the last one belonged to his son and successor Govinda Chandra. The seat of administration of the Chandra rulers was at Vikrampur near Dacca. Before the discovery of these copper plates only four rulers of the dynasty, namely (i) Purna Chandra, (ii) Suvarna Chandra, (iii) Trailokya Chandra; and (iv) Shri Chandra were known. But the newly discovered royal grants give vital information about three more rulers, viz. (i) Kalyana Chandra (ii) Ladaha Chandra (iii) Govinda Chandra to the

succession of Chandra rulers and thus help to complete their genealogy which so long remained incomplete. Their religious faith and imperial position is known from the royal titles adopted by them. The Mainamati plates enable us to suggest with certainty that the Chandra rulers had an uninterrupted succession of rule for a century and a half from 900 A.C. to 1050 A.C.

The fourth copper plate from Charpatra Mura is of a later date. It belongs to a local Hindu Vaishnava ruler Viradhara Deva who issued it as a land grant in his 15th regnal year to the god Shri Vasudeva. The plate shows the Wheel of Vishnu on both sides of the seal. On palaeographical grounds this plate could be assigned to 12th or 13th century A.C.

Terracotta Plaques of Mainamati

The sculptured terracotta plaques decorating the basement wall of central shrine of Salban Vihara form an interesting group, providing excellent specimens of the popular folk art of ancient Bengal. Besides giving a true picture of the social and cultural life of the people, they throw light on the religious practices of the region and the vitality, richness and variety of the Mainamati plaques are striking.

In richness of detail and artistic perfection, these are unique and the variety of subject matter represent-

172

Warrior, terracotta plaque, Mainamati Museum

Rajhansa, terracotta plaque, Mainamati Museum

ed on these panels is overwhelming. All forms of life including men and women, animals and birds, divine and semi-divine beings, composite animals, trees, plants and flowers are represented.

Popular among the animals are the lion, elephant, wild boar and monkeys. The lions are majestic and royal, but the elephants and the wild boars are more successful as naturalistic representations. There are also some fine representations of horses. Among the birds, the Rajhansa is very popular, a tortoise represents the acquatic world while the lotus flower predominates in the plant world.

The dancers and warriors with their characteristic and animated poses are prominent among the human representations. They give us a clear idea of the contemporary dress and ornaments, both male and females. A composite figure occurs frequently among the semi-divine beings. It has a womanish head and bust, bird's wing and animal hind-quarters.

The fighting scene between a large hooded cobra and a comparatively smaller mongoose deserve mention for lively naturalness and movement. Plaques depicting the Dharma-Chakra and Tri-ratna symbols also occur.

Terracotta Plaques of Paharpur

The terracotta plaques of the Paharpur shrine play a most vital part in the scheme of decoration of the walls and there are more than 2000 of them. The richness, variety and exuberance of the plaques from Paharpur are unrivalled and they are dated to the 8th century A.C.

Their subject-matter includes the Buddha; Hindu gods and goddesses; animal fables, dancers, acrobats, warriors, mendicants, ploughmen, musicians, women and children, animals, birds, trees and other objects, sacred or profane, all in bewildering profusion and set in the walls without any coherent sequence. They are well executed, deep-rooted in the folk-art of the countryside and owe little or nothing to academic tradition. These plaques constitute an attractive and distinctive school of popular art of a period in which Buddhism is inextricably mingled with Brahmanical elements.

The fancy and imagination of the terracotta artists of Paharpur are revealed mostly in the various movements of men and women. They are responsive to their environment and every conceivable subject of ordinary human life finds a place in these plaques.

Lion, terracotta plaque, Mainamati Museum

Warrior, terracotta plaque, Mainamati Museum

Hindu Period

TEMPLE ARCHITECTURE

A SYSTEMATIC study of architecture in East Pakistan prior to the advent of the Muslims is rendered difficult by the scarcity of extant standing monuments. Although both internal and external literary evidences and other records abound in testifying to the existence of numerous flourishing cities with magnificent palaces, temples, forts and monasteries before the coming of the Muslims in Bengal, it is strange that no monument of any great pretention, prior to the 13th century, is now in existence above the ground from which the study of their character and artistic qualities could be made. The reasons for such a complete obliteration of Hindu monuments are many, but the most important is the climate. The excessive rainfall during the monsoon encourages the growth of rank vegetation which is a very damaging factor. Added to that is the nature of building materials used in those ancient buildings. East Pakistan's land surface being almost entirely formed of the soft alluvium of rivers, its soft clay provided building material in the shape of burnt bricks, which were laid in mud mortar. This was a highly impermanent binding material fraught with inherent weakness of being washed out.

Among other factors, the constant change of river courses, with disastrous effect, also contributed much to the destruction of many noble monuments of the past.

With such scanty material of the Hindu period we have to depend upon the indirect evidence from sculptures, manuscripts, paintings and excavated remains, in order to reconstruct the form and features of lost monuments. Even in this attempt whatever little information we have, can be gleaned only in relation to the religious buildings, as these were built of more permanent material. Among the Hindu Period architectural remains, temples form the only examples in East Pakistan, and although they belong to the late period of the 16th-18th centuries A.C., yet they stand prominent with their own characteristics and glory.

Ancient temples may be divided into four distinct types. The first and the earliest type consists of a

Gaja-Lakshmi in bronze, Rajshahi Museum

174

Amorous couple in stone, Paharpur Museum

Kanta Nagar temple, Dinajpur

Jor Bangla temple, Pabna

number of horizontal tiers, gradually tapering upwards with a recess between each stage. Later on, in its developed form, the horizontal tiers are compressed into a pyramidal shape. Its design is represented by the Ashrafpur votive bronze Chaitya of 7th century A.C. This early form with its pillars, curvilinear roof and finial, appears nearer to the thatched huts of Bengal.

Side by side with this tiered type, there also developed another type with a lofty tower over the sanctum. The type had much in common with the temples in Orissa. Two other types which are an elaboration of the tiered type are also recognized. In these types, there was a super-structure, either in the shape of a stupa, or of a "Shikhara".

The earliest example is the Govinda Swami temple of Baigram, in Dinajpur district, as mentioned in the Copper Plate Inscription dated 128 Gupta Era. It consisted of a square sanctum, surrounded by an ambulatory passage, and enclosed by a wall with an open terrace on all sides.

Most of the surviving temples in East Pakistan date from the 17th or 18th centuries. They were much influenced by the prevailing Muslim architecture,

especially in respect of surface decoration. Finer examples of this series display exquisite ornamentation in continuous bands of terracotta plaques depicting various subjects from mythology to the ordinary life of the people, against a background of the exuberant scenery of Bengal. The Navaratna Temple at Kantanagar in Dinajpur district, built by Maharaja Pran Nath, and a number of temples of Putia in Rajshahi and of Naldanga in Jessore, are examples of the highest achievement in the plastic art in Bengal. The whole scheme of rich terracotta ornamentation, in figural relief, is skilfully interlaced with beautiful floral, geometric and rosette designs.

The Sarkar Math of Barisal shows general characteristics of spired type, but crowned by a dome with a finial of lotus which is again surmounted by a pitcher with an iron spike protruding above. Other examples of this Shikhara type are the Mathurapur temple of Faridpur and the Kodla Math of Khulna. Another conspicuous example of the same type is the Dacca Race Course Kali Temple built in the 18th century. The temple rises in a lofty conical spire which rests on a raised substructure containing a series of chambers, a feature borrowed from the 18th

Ornamental column, Kanta Nagar temple, Dinajpur

Mother and child, Rajshahi Museum

century Muslim mosques of Khan Mohammad Mirdha and that of Kartalab Khan at Begum Bazar, Dacca.

The Dhakeshwari group of temples at Dacca may be classified under the composite style of terraced and spired pyramid types. Among these, one group of four spired temples rest on a raised platform. Each, having a square sanctum, is capped with six diminishing terraced roof representing the typical curved Bengali type and crowned by a spiked pitcher which is enclosed within a lotus bud. The other group consists of three pyramidal spired temples surmounted by pinnacles. The spires consist of four receding tiers—the first a Bengali domical roof while the remaining three are of the canopied type, and the whole is crowned by a lotus finial.

Another notable architectural feature among the medieval temples is the curvilinear elevation, a typical Bengali element developed obviously from bamboo thatched huts so common in rural Bengal. The cornices of these structures are carried across its front in a series of parallel curves bending in the form of a bow and thus giving a distinctive form to the roof, which is designed to throw off the heavy monsoon rain. One particularly beautiful example of this type is the Bangla temple of Handial in Pabna. The Rajaram temple of Khalia in Faridpur also belongs to this type but it is rectangular in plan and is a two storeyed structure.

Provision of a tower is still another development of this style. A tower is erected over the curved roof, sometimes singly but usually surrounded by a group of corner towers which are richly ornamented with terracotta relief work. According to the number of towers, the temples are classified as five jewelled, nine jewelled and so on. One beautiful example of this jewel type is the seventeen jewelled temple near Comilla, built by the Maharaja of Tripura in the 18th century A.C. Still another variation is the twin-hut type which has a distinctive exterior. As the name suggests, it is a twin structure resembling two thatched bamboo huts joined together. One such beautiful example is the Jor-Bangla temple in Pabna district.

SCULPTURE

The Brahmanical pantheon is of vast complexity in its variety and conception and its iconographic details vary widely from time to time, region to region and text to text. This phase of the lithic art of the 8th-13th centuries A.C. in East Pakistan, to which most of those sculptures belong emerges from the Puranic and Tantric texts instead of the earlier Vedic sources.

The Aryans personified the various manifestations of the forces of nature such as light, fire, wind, sun, storm, rain, etc., as gods and goddesses. The number of these personifications consists chiefly of three i.e., fire on earth, wind in the air and the sun in heaven and these personifications are recognized in the icons of Agni, Indra and Surya. However, in the course of later evolutions, these Vedic deities were relegated to less important positions with the ushering in of a multitude of Puranic divinities when Brahma, Vishnu and Shiva came into prominence. Hence we find the Puranic triad of Brahma, Vishnu and Shiva representing the Creator, the Preserver and the Destroyer respectively in place of the Vedic triad of Agni, Indra and Surya. Again, by the time these conceptions were given lithic form, Brahma was discarded from worship. Vishnu and Shiva in their various forms together with Surya, in lesser degree, became the chief icons of the Brahmanical pantheon, while their wives and children now share among themselves the

*Krishna killing
...hin or Dhenuka,
...harpur Museum*

Decorated column, Mahasthangarh Museum

Yama in stone, Paharpur Museum

in the current Tantric texts. As such, the identifications of the images cannot always be regarded as certain.

The most popular god in East Pakistan, was Vishnu whose image is by far the most numerous. Next to him, in order of popularity, is the sun-god, Surya. The Varmans and the Senas, the two powerful Brahmanical royal families who ruled the eastern and the whole of Bengal respectively were staunch adherents of these two gods.

Most of the images of Vishnu are accompanied by his two wives Sarasvati, the goddess of culture and learning who stands to his left, and Lakshmi, the goddess of beauty and wealth who stands to his right. Garuda, the vehicle of the god, is always represented below the lotus seat. The usual attributes of Vishnu are the conch-shell, wheel, mace and lotus and he is highly ornamented. Representations of the ten incarnations of Vishnu, viz., fish, tortoise, boar, man-lion, dwarf, Rama, Parashurama, Balarama, Buddha and Kalki are also met with on the two sides of the main figure. Among the individual representations, the dwarf incarnation of Vishnu is important. He is represented with four hands holding the wheel, mace, lotus and conch-shell respectively. His left leg is raised towards the sky and the four-armed figure of Brahma is represented over his raised leg. The scene of Bali's gift is depicted below the central figure.

Although the worship of the sun-god, Surya, has practically disappeared from East Pakistan, it was evidently at one time a very popular deity next only to Vishnu, as is testified by the abundance of images from the 8th to the 13th centuries A.C.

Shaivism flourished in Bengal during the rule of the powerful Sena kings who accepted the cult and the ten-armed figure of Shiva was adopted on their royal seal.

The Tantric texts evolved a complicated Shiva iconography which conceived various forms of the god and correspondingly, images in numerous forms of Shiva were readily carved by the local sculptors. Among the chief forms of the Shiva image found in East Pakistan are ten or twelve armed Nataraja, dancing on his mount, Nandi Bull. The representation of Shiva in the anthropomorphic form of half-man and half-woman is indeed unparalleled.

Another very interesting representation is the embracing Shiva in which he is shown on a lotus throne with right leg pendant and his wife sitting on his tucked up left leg. The god and the goddess are represented as embracing each other.

The Brahmanical pantheon of goddesses is divided into two groups; the Vaishnavi and the Shakti. Shakti is the female counter-part of Shiva and in

worship of the Hindus. Incidentally, it should be mentioned that considering the wide variations of attributes of the gods and goddesses in East Pakistan with those of the rest of the sub-continent, it appears that the East Pakistani artists probably were guided by an altogether separate set of art-manuals from the rest. This is evident from the fact that many images of East Pakistan do not correspond to any known iconographic texts and, curiously enough, several icons bearing definite names given in inscribed pedestals, do not exactly fit in their descriptions given

Hara-Gauri in stone, Rajshahi Museum

Images of Ganesha are rather common in East Pakistan. He is usually represented with four hands sitting on a lotus seat with one leg pendant. In his four hands he holds rosary, trident, lotus and sweet respectively. His vehicle, the rat, is always represented below and generally he is much bejewelled.

Stone Sculptures of Paharpur

The basement wall of the temple of Paharpur is embellished with sixty three stone-reliefs of varying character and quality, and probably they represent very fairly the general range of local sculpture in the 7th and 8th centuries A.C. They include only one Buddhist image, a Bodhisattva fronted by a small tank. For the rest, they represent a number of Brahmanical or even secular figures and groups, with a special emphasis on the Krishna legend. These can broadly be divided into three groups; (1) a series of panels in delicate hieratic style, recalling the academic tradition of the late Gupta period, (2) a large number of relatively crude sculptures, in a heavy but lively style, essentially akin to that of folk-art, and (3) a series which may be described as a compromise between the two. Whether these stylistic differences represent a variety of contemporary schools or whether they are due to the re-use of earlier sculptures alongside work contemporary with the building, is a moot point, but the latter alternative is the more probable. It seems likely that a nucleus of derived late Gupta reliefs was reset in the present structure and was liberally supplemented by local village artists who sometimes tried to stimulate the traditional hieratic manner.

The first group of these stone reliefs exhibits the somewhat vapid elegance of the evolved Gupta classicism. Details of ornament are rendered with minute precision, and human forms have a conventional grace, with attenuated limbs and clinging lifeless drapery. Subjects include the traditional lovers, Krishna and Radha, Yamuna standing on a tortoise, and Balarama with snake-hood and plough.

The second group consists of high reliefs, representing a variety of scenes and figures in a vigorous style which is often heavy and lacking in knowledge but nevertheless expressive in a naive but direct manner. It displays no spiritual or intellectual quality. The features are roughly differentiated and the drapery is indicated in summery simplicity. But it is a vivid and convincing snapshot of the life of the village and of the gods and monsters which peopled the village-mind. Its expressiveness is in proportion to its lack of academic learning or metaphysical content. Its subjects are often taken from the life of Krishna whose amorous and other adventures were so dear to the Bengali heart. Others are borrowed

Tantric literature, the latter is active only with the former. That the conception of the Shakti as the female counter-part or the female energy of the god without whose active co-operation the god is powerless, was well established. The goddesses Lakshmi and Sarasvati were assigned as the Shaktis of Vishnu, and Parvati of Shiva. Most of the forms of these Shakti images are fierce in character except those of Lakshmi and Sarasvati who are represented with pleasant youthful faces, accompanying Vishnu on his right and left respectively.

The representation of "the Mother and Child" is a very fine specimen of lithic art found particularly in North Bengal. In this representation, the mother is shown lying down on a couch. She holds a lotus in her right hand while the left one rests on the pillow supporting the head on the palm. A maid is represented shampooing one of her legs and a child is shown lying down by the side of the mother. Two more maids with fans and fly-whisks are placed on both sides of the couch. The gods Kartikeya and Ganesha and also a linga are shown above.

General view of central temple, Paharpur

Kalyana Sundara in stone, Bogra, Rajshahi Museum   *Vishnu in bronze, Rajshahi Museum*

Khadiravani Tara, Rajshahi, Rajshahi Museum

Nativity of the Buddha, Dinajpur, Rajshahi Museum

from the epics which held a high place in the affections of the countryside. Dancers and other figures familiar to the social and religious life of the village are included.

The third group of sculptures is a compromise between the hieratic and the folk art and is less satisfactory.

COINS

Coins of the Hindu period in East Pakistan are very rare, but whatever have been found are mostly of gold or silver. One gold coin found at Mainamati was issued by Samudragupta, 340 A.C.—380 A.C., on the occasion of the Horse Sacrifice to celebrate his conquest of India. On the obverse, a horse is depicted while on the reverse the figure of the king is enclosed by a legend in Brahmi script. Another coin belonging to Chandragupta II, 380 A.C.—414 A.C. is of Lakshmi and Archer type. Besides these, quite a number of gold coins in imitation of the Gupta coins, but without any legend, were found from Mainamati and were issued by one of the local dynasties of the area. Another group of gold coins, also in imitation of the imperial Gupta, depicting the standing figure of the king, with the legend 'Valabhatta' on the obverse and a dotted figural representation with garland around on the reverse, is significant. The king on the obverse is faced by a couchant bull. One of the copper plate inscriptions of Mainamati shows the bull representation in the royal emblem and the same was issued by a Shaiva prince named Valabhatta. The occurrence of the name of Valabhatta on the coins as well as on the copper plate along with the same emblem of couchant bull significantly indicates the existence of a powerful Shaiva dynasty in the region of Samatata in the 6th-7th centuries A.C.

Mainamati excavation also yielded a silver coin of Shashanka, early 7th century A.C., showing the representation of Shiva on the reverse and the cross-legged king on the obverse.

MINOR ARTS

Miscellaneous minor arts, belonging to Hindu period in East Pakistan include beautiful buttons, ear-drops, pendants and nose-studs of various materials and shape. They range from terracotta to several varieties of semi-precious stones such as agate, cornelian, lapis-lazuli, marble, crystal, glass, chalcedony, onyk, white opal, faience, etc., terracotta figurines and toys and copper antimony rods, ring and bangles.

Other datable objects include a circular flat clay seal bearing three stalks of a wheat plant united at the lower and enclosed by an inscription with 22 Brahmi letters on the margin. There is an exquisitely modelled terracotta female head wearing a crown. Both the seal and the female head are assignable to the golden age of the Guptas—4th century A.C. More than a dozen Sunga plaques depicting the Mother Goddess in her characteristic modelling, datable to the 2nd-1st century B.C. and a beautiful circular disc of blue-schist, engraved in low relief with a panel depicting deer, a tiger, an elephant, alternated by pitchers issuing festooned scrolls, which may be dated to 1st-2nd centuries A.C. from the earlier Hindu levels of Mahasthangarh are also important.

The Sunga terracotta plaques depict a female figure with elaborate head-dress, bedecked richly with ornaments and, usually, one hand resting on hip and the other holding her girdle of flowers. The figure, evidently represents a goddess, as is clear from one of the plaques where she is attended by a kneeling female devotee with an offering in her hand. Usually, four weapons, namely, trident, thunderbolt, elephant-goad and arrow are depicted on either side of the head. Among other plaques of the same period, a beautiful piece, depicting three elephants with a female "Chawri" bearer standing alongside and a chariot drawn by three horses, is noteworthy.

Among the stone objects, a fragmentary square black-stone, with the image of Vishnu on one side and his ten incarnations on the other, several fragments of blue schist medallions, jeweller's moulds for ornaments, an image of Nandi Bull in black stone and a beautiful ring-stone and toilet tray are prominent.

Metal objects include copper rings, bangles, antimony rods, a copper medallion, an iron spear-head, knife, razor, nails, a collection of octo-alloy bangles and an ornamental amulet.

Glossary

Adi Buddha the Universal Father in Buddhist hierarchy of gods.

Adi Prajna the Universal Mother in Buddhist hierarchy of gods.

Agni vedic fire god.

Aitareya Brahmana name of a Brahmana composed by the sage Aitareya.

Akshobhya the second meditative Buddha, "the immovable one".

Amitabha the fourth meditative Buddha, "of unmeasured splendour".

Amoghasiddhi the name of the fifth meditative Buddha, "one whose accomplishment is unerring".

Amphora a two-handled vessel for holding wine and oil.

Ananda one of the most favourite disciples of the Buddha.

Archway an arched or vaulted passage.

Ashoka-kanta one of the female attendants of the Buddhist goddess Shyama Tara.

Athsho an Iranian metal god.

Avalokiteshvara the Great Lord of Mercy in Buddhism.

Balarama name of the elder brother of Krishna and regarded as the eighth incarnation of Vishnu.

Bali name of a demon-king who was humiliated by Vishnu in the form of a dwarf.

Balustrade a rod of small vertical pillars with base and rail forming a protective enclosure.

Base-relief a low relief or carving.

Bhangra dance a typical Punjabi dance performed on festive occasions.

Bharhut a village with a famous ancient Buddhist site about 95 miles south-west of Allahabad, India.

Bhrikuti-Tara a Buddhist goddess emanating from the Meditative Buddha Amitabha and a companion of Avalokiteshvara.

Billion a base metal of silver with copper, tin or the like.

Bodhgaya a sacred place of Buddhist pilgrimage in Bihar in India where Buddha attained enlightenment.

Bodhisattva Buddha before the enlightenment.

Bodhi-tree Tree of Wisdom under which Buddha obtained the Buddha-hood.

Bone awl a boring tool made of bone, one end of which was fitted into a handle.

Boulder a large weather-worn block of stone.

Brahma the absolute creator of all things. Chief of the Hindu Trinity with Vishnu and Shiva.

Bronze Age the period in history which succeeded the Neolithic Age and when tools and weapons were made chiefly of bronze though stone tools were still used.

Buddha the enlightened one.

Butkara an ancient Buddhist site in Swat State in West Pakistan.

Calcareous sandstone sand stone containing lime.

Canyon deep gorge or ravine with steep sides, at the bottom of which a river flows.

Cell a small room used by the monks in a monastery.

Cella the main body of a temple.

Cellular building with a number of cells or small apartments.

Celt a term for a chisel or axe-head made of stone, bronze or iron.

Chalcedony a semi-precious stone with various tints.

Chawri fly-whisk.

Chert a type of rock used for tool-making in Palaeolithic times.

Chevron an angle-shaped decorative design.

Chequer division into square like chess-board.

Chopper a short handled but large bladed axe.

Chunda one of the Buddhist esoteric goddesses emanating from Meditative Buddha "Vairochana".

Cinquefoil an ornament with five cuspidated divisions.

Cloison partition or division.

Colonade a series of columns forming the side of a narrow path of a building.

Concave, a form which curves inward. It is thicker around the edge and tapers towards the centre where it becomes considerably thinner.

Cone conical shaped terracotta objects used for decorative purposes.

Conglomerate a composite rock consisting of rounded and water-worn fragments.

Conical spire cone-shaped finial.

Corbel a projection of brick or stone, jutting out from the face of a wall to support a superincumbent weight.

Cordon an ornamental motif in the form of a cord.

Core a Palaeolithic tool which was made by chipping flakes from a piece of flint.

Corinthian pilasters thin, rectangular and ornate piers projecting from the face of a wall, as used in classical period in Corinth, Greece.

Cornelian a semi-precious stone of deep dull red, flesh or reddish white colour.

Convex a form which curves out from the centre. It is thick in the centre and tapers out at the edge.

Cruciform a cross-shaped form.

Cupola a spherical vault.

Curvilinear roof a roof having a bow like curved lines under the parapet.

Cylindrical drum barrel-shaped part of a stupa under the dome.

Dasyus enemy of the gods. The Aryans called the original inhabitants of the sub-continent by this name.

Deer-Park also known as "Mirgadava" at Sarnath near Benares where the Buddha preached his first sermon after enlightenment.

Devas the gods.

Dharma the law, one of the three

jewels of Buddhism.

Dharma-Chakra the Wheel of Law, a symbol of Buddhism.

Dharma-Vijaya this legend occurs on some of the silver coins found at Mainamati. "Conquest by Law".

Diaper chequered patterns in stone.

Diaphanous dress transparent dress.

Diorama a mode of scenic representation of life.

Ekajata one of the female companions of the Buddhist goddess Shyama Tara. She is usually represented with a knife and a skull in her hands.

Faience material which is composed of a white or greyish paste coated with a glaze.

Filigree jewel work of a delicate kind made with threads, and beads usually of gold and silver.

Finial an ornamental projection at the apex of a temple or a stupa.

Flake a stone tool, knapped off a lump, nodule, pebble or core.

Flint blade a cutting instrument made of a hard bluish-grey rock.

Fluted handle a handle ornamented with a flute-like design.

Gaja-Lakshmi a Hindu goddess of fortune attended on either side by two water pouring elephants.

Ganesha a Hindu god of success represented with an elephant head and four arms.

Garuda the Vehicle of Vishnu, represented as a powerfully built man with two wings and having some bird like features in the face.

Goblet a drinking cup without handles, sometimes mounted on a foot.

Granite igneous unstratified hard rock consisting of quartz, felspar and mica.

Grave culture newly found cemeteries in Dir and Swat which present a pattern of living between the end of the Indus culture and the beginning of the historic period in the 6th century B.C.

Great Master The Buddha.

Hara-Gauri Hindu god Shiva and goddess Parvati when represented together.

Hariti a Buddhist goddess of fertility and protector of children.

Harmika railed balcony surmounting the dome of a Buddhist stupa. "Pavilion".

Hatched a design motif with engraved or applied lines.

Hayagriva a Buddhist god who is a defender of the Faith and an emanation from Buddha Akshobhya.

Helios The Greek Sun-god.

Herakles a Greek god of strength and power.

Harpocrates a Greek child-god worshipped in Alexandria in the early centuries of the Christian era.

Heruka one of the most popular esoteric deities of the Buddhist pantheon, the destroyer of all the worldly mischieves, emanated from meditative Buddha Akshobhya.

Hevajra a Buddhist god Heruka with his spouse.

Hexagon a polygonal form with six sides.

Hinayana early Buddhism with emphasis on the doctrine rather than on the worship of the Buddha. "The Little Vehicle".

Indra the Vedic god of the atmosphere and sky.

Indrashala a noted cave in the Buddhist mythology.

Inflexed burial extended practice of burial of the dead.

Interglacial warm or a temperate climate intervening the period of glaciation or Ice-Age.

Jambhala Buddhist god of wealth.

Jasper a kind of precious stone.

Kalachakra one of the Buddhist gods, an emanation of meditative Buddha Akshobhya.

Kalyana Sundara an image which depicts the marriage scene of Shiva and Parvati.

Kanjur stone local name of a soft limestone used at Taxila.

Kartikeya son of Parvati, a Hindu god.

Khadga dynasty a Buddhist dynasty ruling over south-east Bengal during 6th-7th century A.C.

Khadiravani-Tara also known as Shyama Tara. One of the goddesses of Buddhist pantheon.

Kharoshthi an old script used in the north-western parts of the subcontinent between the 3rd century B.C. and 5th century A.C.

Khatvanga a type of club surmounted either by a thunderbolt, skull, trident or the banner.

Khwar a river-bed.

King Shuddhodana father of the Buddha.

Krishna name of a celebrated incarnation of Vishnu, represented as a young and amorous shepherd sporting with the Gopis or shepherdesses.

Kushinagara a place in Nepal where the Buddha breathed his last.

Kuvera a Hindu god of wealth and the guardian of the North. He is also the chief of the Yakshas.

Lakshmi spouse of Vishnu, goddess of fortune and wealth.

Linga a phallic symbol representing the Hindu god Shiva.

Loops a curving design.

Lumbini garden a place in Nepal where the Buddha was born.

Mahakala one of the many terrible deities of the Buddhist pantheon represented as the Defenders of Faith.

Mahamaya a Hindu goddess representing the source of all the manifestations of the universe.

Mahayana later theistic form of Buddhism with emphasis on the divine Buddhas and Bodhisattvas. "The Great Vehicle".

Maitreya the Buddha of the future who will come to earth for the deliverance of all beings.

Mala a garland.

Manjushri a Buddhist god of learning and culture.

Mara personification of evil spirits in Buddhism.

Marichi a Buddhist goddess of dawn emanating from meditative Buddha 'Vairochana'.

Megalithic stones huge blocks indicating burials erected during the Neolithic and early Bronze periods.

Micro-blades small chipped and worked blades used in the Mesolithic Age.

Middle Stone Age Mesolithic age when man led a semi-nomadic life.

Mongoloid people with Mongolian features.

Mother goddess the goddess of fertility whose cult was popular in the Indus Valley and near Middle East in ancient times.

Nagarjuna a magician and master of esoteric studies and one of the chief propagators of the Buddhist faith.

Nana an Iranian goddess of spring and fertility.

Nandi Bull the vehicle of Shiva.

Nataraja Shiva in dancing pose.

Navaratna Temple nine-jewelled temple so called for its nine spires, at Kanta Nagar, Dinajpur, East Pakistan.

Neolithic The New Stone Age characterized by the development of agriculture and domestication of animals.

Niche a window like cavity in the

wall for the reception of images and oil lamps.

Nimbus a disk at the back of the Buddha's head.

Nirvana death of the Buddha.

Nodules a stony formation in soil due to deposition of calcium carbonates.

Oado the Iranian wind-god.

Octo-alloy an alloy of eight metals used for bronze images.

Onyx a precious gem stone with brown, white or black concentric bands.

Opal a precious gem-stone with various fiery play of colours like red, green and blue.

Padmasambhava one of the deified personages in Buddhist Pantheon as Defender of Faith.

Pagodas a variety of Buddhist stupa found in South East Asia.

Panchika a Buddhist god of fertility and the protector of children.

Pan-na-fa-tan-na pundravardhana as called by Hiuen Tsang.

Pannier a cup shaped head dress on either side of the head of mother-goddess figurines.

Parnashavari a Buddhist goddess who prevents epidemics.

Parashurama an incarnation of Vishnu.

Pattikera an ancient kingdom of south-east Bengal.

Pellets tiny balls used in decorative works like terracotta human figurine.

Phyllite a rock consisting an argillaceous schist or slate containing scales or flakes of mica.

Pit a cavity in the ground either natural or formed by digging.

Pleistocene the first sub-division of the Quaternary period which covers the four Glacial Periods of the Great Ice Age.

Podium a continuous low pedestal supporting a number of columns.

Po-shi-po Vasu Vihara as called by Hiuen Tsang.

Prajnaparamita the Primeval Mother in the Buddhist pantheon.

Proto-Austra-loid an early people with dominant Australian features.

Proto-Europoid an early racial stock with prominent European features.

Pundras the original inhabitants of north Bengal as mentioned in the Vedic literatures.

Pundravardhana-Bhukti ancient sub-division of Bengal corresponding with the northern districts of East Pakistan.

Quartz a silica mineral with chemical composition as Silican Dioxide found in crystalline form. It is the most common mineral in sedimentary rocks and sand.

Quartzite sand or other siliceous minerals hardened into rocky masses.

Quatrefoil a tracery panel with four foils and cusps.

Queen Maya mother of the Buddha.

Radha beloved of Krishna.

Rajhansa "swan".

Rama the hero of the Ramayana and an incarnation of Vishnu.

Ratna-Sambhava an esoteric Buddhist god.

Relic Casket a casket for depositing the bones or ashes of the Buddha or his disciples.

Repousse ornamented relief work by means of hammering from the reverse side.

Rigveda a sacred religious book of the Hindus.

Roundels a form in art with circular designs.

Saddlequern a grinding stone.

Sakyamuni the Buddha. "The sage of the Sakya race".

Samatata an ancient sub-division of Bengal corresponding with the districts lying on the eastern side of the Meghna river.

Sangha monastery, one of the three jewels of Buddhism.

Sapta Sindhu the territories watered by the rivers Kabul, Indus, Beas, Sutlej, Jhelum, Chenab and Ravi. "The Seven Indus".

Sarasvati a Hindu goddess of learning and culture, one of the spouses of Vishnu.

Sarvani one of the forms of Hindu goddess Durga.

Satrapy an administrative sub-division of the Achaemenids.

Schist a kind of rock formation consisting metamorphosed shale.

Scraper a palaeolithic stone tool used for scraping hides and skins.

Selene the moon-goddess of Greek pantheon.

Shakti the active power of a god and the creative force in its feminine aspect.

Shakya family the race in which the Buddha was born.

Shikara a typical form of Hindu architecture. "Spire".

Shitatapatra a form of the Buddhist goddess Tara.

Shiva one of the gods of Hindu trinity.

Shyama Tara a goddess of the Buddhist pantheon emanating from meditative Buddha Akshobhya, also known as Khadiravani-Tara.

Steatite a variety of talc stone.

Stone Age the age of human development in which stone was used as weapons and implements.

Stucco a fine plaster composed of gypsum and pulverized marble.

Stupa Buddhist relic mound, erected over the body relic of the Buddha or his disciples.

Sunga a Brahmanical dynasty succeeding the Mauryans (185 B.C.—75 B.C.).

Surya the sun-god.

Swastika an ancient auspicious symbol.

Takshasila Sanskritized form of Taxila.

Tantric blending of Buddhist and Hindu elements. "Esoteric".

Tara the consort of Bodhisattva.

Taranath the Tibetan historian of 16th-17th centuries A.C.

Terracotta art objects made of burnt clay. "Burnt Earth".

Tiara "crown".

Torque a characteristic broad necklace like gold ornament used by the Scytho-Parthians.

Traystrimsa Heaven the thirty-third heaven where the Buddha lived before his descent on to the earth.

Tripitaka Buddhist religious book consisting of three pitakas or parts.

Tri-ratna three jewels of Buddhism represented by a trident—Buddha, Dharma and Sanga.

Tunic a garment resembling a shirt worn by both sexes among the Greeks and Romans.

Urn Burial a system of depositing the remains of a dead in a jar for burial purpose.

Urna curl of hair between the eyebrows of the Buddha.

Unicorn a mythical animal with a single horn depicted on seals of Mohenjodaro and Harappa.

Ushnisha over head protruberance formed by hair of the Buddha.

Vairochana one of the five meditative Buddhas in the pose of turning the Wheel of Law.

Vaishnavaite the followers of Vishnu.

Vajrapani an attendant of the Buddha in Gandhara sculpture. "The Thunderbolt Bearer".

Vajra-Tara one of the forms of the Buddhist goddess Tara emanating from meditative Buddha Ratnasambhava.

Vajrasattva an active agent of the Adi Buddha.

Varendra ancient name of north Bengal.

Vasu-Vihara a stupa about 4 miles west of Mahasthangarh said to be built by Ashoka.

Vedas the sacred Hindu books.

Vina a stringed musical instrument.

Vinaya an important text of the Buddhist religious book Tripitaka.

Visage urns a burial jar representing a human face.

Vishnu one of the gods of Hindu trinity.

Vitapala a celebrated sculpture of Bengal during the Pala period.

Votive stupa a stupa built as a work of great religious merit by the Buddhist devotees at the centres of pilgrimage.

Voussoir a wedge shaped stone or brick for an arch.

Wheel of Law Dharma-Chakra, the symbol of Buddhist belief.

Wheel of Vishnu Vishnu-chakra, an attribute of Vishnu.

White Huns a militant nomadic central Asian horde who invaded the Gandhara region in 5th century A.C.

Yab-Yum pose of the Buddhist god Hevajra embracing his spouse.

Yakshas the male tree-spirits in both Hinduism and Buddhism.

Yakshis the female tree-spirits in both Hinduism and Buddhism.

Yama the god of death.

Yamapukur-Brata a ritual practice performed by the Hindu maidens of Bengal for long life and prosperity of their families and themselves for four consecutive years from mid-October to mid-November.

Yashodhara the wife of the Buddha.

Yoni the female organ represented with the Shiva-lingam.

Bibliography

Ancient India. Bulletin of the Archaeological Survey of India, Delhi, Department of Archaeology, 1946.

Basham, A.L. *The wonder that was India*. A survey of the culture of the Indian sub-continent before the coming of the Muslims. London, Sidgwick and Jackson, 1961.

Bhattacharyya, B. *The Indian Buddhist iconography*. 2nd ed. Mainly based on the Sadhanamala and Cognatic Tantric Text of the Rituals, Calcutta, Firma K.L. Mukhopadhyay, 1958.

Bhattacharyya, Haridas, ed. *The cultural heritage of India*. In four volumes. Introduction by Bharataratna Bhagavan, Calcutta, Ramakrishna Mission Institute of Culture, 1956.

Bhattasali, N.K. *Iconography of Buddhist and Brahmanical sculptures in the Dacca Museum*. With preface by H.E. Stepleton. Dacca, 1929.

Birdwood, George C.M. *The industrial arts of India*. With map and woodcuts. In two volumes. London, Chapman and Hall, 1880.

Blacker, J.F. *ABC of Indian art*. London, Stanley Paul & Co., 1922.

Brown, P. *Indian architecture (Buddhist and Hindu periods)*. With drawings, photographs and maps. Bombay, D.B. Taraporevala & Sons, 1942.

Bussagli, Mario. *Gandhara, Encyclopaedia of World Art*, Vol. VI, pp. 18-35. London, McGraw Hill, 1962.

Cambridge History of India. Vol. 1. Edited by E. J. Rapson. Cambridge University Press. 1922.

Casal, J.M. *Fouilles D' Amri*. Two volumes. Paris, Librairie C. Klincksieck, 1964.

Childe, V. Gordon. *New light on the most ancient East*. London, Routledge & Kegan Paul, 1952.

Coomarswamy, Ananda K. *Arts and crafts of India and Ceylon*. London, T.N. Fouilis, 1913.

Cousens, H. *Antiquities of Sind*. With historical outlines, Calcutta, Government of India Central Publication Branch, 1929.

Cunningham, Alexander. *Ancient geography of India*. I. The Buddhist period including the campaigns of Alexander and the travels of Hiuen-Tsang. London, Trubner & Co., 1871.

Dani, A.H. *Buddhist sculpture in East Pakistan*. Karachi, Department of Archaeology, 1959.

Dani, A.H. *The Gandhara art of Pakistan* (Mss.).

Dani, A.H. *Sanghao cave excavation*. Ancient Pakistan, 1964. Vol. 1, pp. 1-50.

Dani, A.H. *Timargarha and Gandhara grave culture*. Ancient Pakistan, 1967. Vol. 3.

Day, Lal Behari. *Govinda Samanta or the history of a Bengal Raiyat*. London, Macmillan and Co. 1874.

Dikshit, K.N. *Excavations at Paharpur, Bengal*. Archaeological Survey of India, Memoir No. 55, Delhi, 1938.

Dikshit, S.K. *Problem of the Kusanas and the origin of the Vikrama Samvat*.
Annals of the Bhandarkar Oriental Research Institute:—
Vol. 33, pp. 114-170.
Vol. 34, pp. 70-112.
Vol. 38, pp. 93-114.

D'Oyley and Landseer, J. *Antiquities of Dacca*. London, 1827.

Fairservis, Walter A. *Excavations in the Quetta Valley, West Pakistan*. New York, American Museum of Natural History, 1956.

Foucher, A. *The Beginning of Buddhist art and other essays in India and Central Asian Archaeology*. Paris, Paul Geuthner, 1917.

Gadd, C.J. *Seals of ancient Indian style found at Ur*. London, Proceeding of British Academy, 1932. Vol. 18.

Garratt, G.T. ed. *The legacy of India*. With an introduction by the Marquess of Zetland. Oxford, Clarendon Press, 1938.

Gode, P.K. *Studies in Indian Cultural history*. In three volumes. Hoshiarpur, Vishveshvaranand Vedic Research Institute, 1961.

Gokhale, H.G. *Ancient India: history and culture*. Bombay, Asia Publishing House, 1959.

Gordon, D.H. *The pottery industries of the Indo-Iranian border*. Ancient India, 1954-55, Nos. 10-11, pp. 157-191.

Gordon, D.H. *The pre-historic background of Indian culture*. 2nd ed. Bombay, N.M. Tripathi, 1960.

Gordon, D.H. *The Stone industries of the Holocene in India and Pakistan*. Ancient India, 1950, No. 6, pp. 64-90.

Grunwedel, Albert. *Buddhist art in India*. Translated from the 'Handbuch' of Prof. Albert Grunwedel, by Agnes C. Gibson. Revised and enlarged by Jas Burgess. London, Bernard Quaritch, 1901.

Hargreaves. *Handbook to the sculptures in the Peshawar Museum*. Calcutta, Central Publication Branch, 1930.

Hargreaves, H. *Notes on the ancient geography of Gandhara*. Calcutta, Superintendent of Government Printing, 1915.

Havell, E.B. *Ancient and mediaeval architecture of India: a study of Indo-Aryan civilization*. London, John Murray, 1915.

Hawkes, Jacquetta and others. *Palaeolithic human industries in the North West Punjab and Kashmir and their geological significance* by J. Hawkes, C. Hawkes, and H. De Terra. Connecticut Acad. Arts and Sci. Mem., vol. 8, 1934.

Heine-Geldern, R. *The Coming of the Aryans and the end of the Harappa civilization*. London, Macmillan and Co. 1910.

Holdich, Sir Thomas. *The Gates of India—being an historical narrative*. With maps. London, Man, Vol. 56, 1956.

Holdich, Sir Thomas Hunderford.

India. London, Henry Frowde.

Hunter, W.W. *The Indian empire: its people, history, and products.* 2nd ed. London, Trubner & Co. 1886.

Indian Archaeology (an annual). New Delhi, Government of India. Ministry of Education, 1953-61.

Ingholt, H. *The Gandharan art in Pakistan.* New York, 1957.

Khan, F.A. *Banbhore.* Karachi, Department of Archaeology, 1963.

Khan, F.A. *The glory that was Harappa* Karachi, Department of Archaeology, 1967.

Khan, F.A. *The glory that was Mohenjodaro.* Karachi, Department of Archaeology, 1966.

Khan, F.A. *The Indus Valley and Early Iran.* Karachi. Department of Archaeology, 1964.

Khan, F.A. *Mainamati.* Karachi, Department of Archaeology, 1963.

Khan, F.A. *Preliminary Report on Kot Diji Excavations, 1957-58.* Karachi, Department of Archaeology.

Kohli, Sita Ram. *The Indus Valley civilization: Being a summary of three extension lectures delivered at Patiala.* Lahore, Albert Press, 1934.

Kosambi, D.D. *The Culture and civilisation of ancient India in Historical outline.* London, Routledge and Kegan Paul, 1965.

Kramrisch, S. *The art of India; traditions of Indian sculpture, painting and architecture.* London, The Phaidon Press, 1954.

Kramrisch, Stella. *The Hindu Temple.* In two volumes. Photographs by Raymond Burnier. Calcutta University, Calcutta, 1946.

Krishnaswami, V.D. *Stone age India.* Ancient India, 1947, No. 3. pp. 11-58.

Latif, S.M. *Lahore: its history, architectural remains and antiquities.* With an account of its modern institutions, inhabitants, their trade, customs & c. Lahore, New Imperial Press, 1892.

Lohuizen-de-Leeuw, J.E. Van. *The 'Scythian' Period. An approach to the history, art, epigraphy and palaeography of North India from the 1st century B.C. to the 3rd century A.D.* Leiden, E.J. Brill, 1949.

Lowenthal, W. *Account of some sculptures in the Peshawar Museum.* Journal of the Asiatic Society of Bengal, 1862, vol. 31. p. 411.

Mackay, E.J.H. *Chanhu-Daro Excavations, 1935-36.* Published for American School of India and Iranian studies and Museum of Fine Arts Boston. New Haven, American Oriental Society, 1943.

Mackay, Ernest. *Early Indus civilisation.* 2nd ed. revised and enlarged by Dorothy Mackay. London, Luzac & Co., 1948.

Majumdar, R.C. *The classical accounts of India.* Being a compilation of the English translation of the account left by Herodotus, Magasthenese, Arrian, Starbo, Quintus Diodorus, Siculus ... Calcutta, Firma K.L. Mukhopadhyay, 1960.

Majumdar, R.C. ed. *History of Bengal.* Vol. I. Hindu Period. Dacca University, 1963.

Majumdar, R.C. ed. *History and culture of the Indian people.* vol. 1-4. London, George Allen & Unwin.

Marshall, Sir John. *The Buddhist Art of Gandhara.* London, Department of Archaeology, Pakistan, 1960.

Marshall, Sir John. *A guide to Taxila.* 4th ed. Cambridge University Press, 1960.

Marshall, Sir John. *Mohenjodaro and the Indus civilisation.* Being an official account of Archaeological Excavations at Mohenjodaro carried out by the Government of India between the years 1922 and 1927. In three volumes with plan and map in colours and 164 plates in collotype. London, Arthur Probsthain, 1931.

Marshall, Sir John. *Taxila; an illustrated account of Archaeological Excavations carried out at Taxila under the orders of the Government of India between the years 1913 and 1934.* In three volumes. Cambridge University Press, 1951.

M'Crindle, J.W. *Ancient India as described in classical literature.* Being a collection of Greek and Latin texts relating to India, extracted from Herodotus, Starbo, Diodorus Siculus, Pliny, Aelian ... Translated and copiously annotated by J.W. M'Crindle. Westminster, Archibald Constable & Co., 1901.

Mehta, Ratilal N. *Pre-Buddhist India; A political administrative, economic, social and geographical survey of Ancient India based mainly on the Jataka Stories.* Bombay, Examiner Press, 1939.

Mitra, Rajendralala. *Indo-Aryans: Contribution towards the elucidation of their ancient and mediaeval History,* In two volumes. Calcutta, W. Newman & Co., 1881.

Mode, Heinz. *Das Fruhe Indian.* Stuttgart, Gustav Kilpper Verlag, 1959.

Monahan, F.J. *The Early History of Bengal.* Oxford, 1925.

Mukerjee, Radhakamal. *The Culture and art of India.* London, George Allen and Unwin, 1959.

Nazimuddin Ahmed. *Mahasthan. A Preliminary Report on the Recent Archaeological Excavations at Mahasthangarh.* Karachi, Department of Archaeology, 1964.

Pakistan Archaeology, No. 1-3. Karachi, Department of Archaeology, 1964-66.

Pakistan, Department of Archaeology. *Gandhara Sculpture in the National Museum of Pakistan.* Karachi, 1964.

Panikkar, K.M. *A Survey of Indian history.* 3rd ed. Bombay, Asian Publishing House, 1956.

Paterson, T.T. & Drummond, H.J.H. *Soan the palaeolithic of Pakistan.* Karachi, Department of Archaeology, 1962.

Paul, Pramode Lal. *The Early History of Bengal (From the earliest times to the Muslim conquest.)* With a foreword by R.C. Majumdar. Calcutta, Indian Research Institute, 1939.

Piggot, Stuart. *Prehistoric India.* London, 1962.

Powell-Price, J.C. *History of India.* London, Thomas Nelson and Sons, 1955.

Ramachandran, T.N. *Recent Archaeological discoveries along the Mainamati and Lalmai Ranges, Tipera District, East Bengal, in B.C. Law Volume, Part II.* pp. 213-231. Poona, Bhandarkar Research Institute, 1946.

Rao, S.R. *The Excavation at Lothal.* Lalit Kala, 1956-57. No. 3-4.

Rawlinson, H.G. *India: A short cultural history.* Edited by C.G. Selligman. London, Cresset Press, 1937.

Rawlinson, H.G. *Intercourse between India and the Western world from the earliest time to the fall of Rome.* Cambridge University Press, 1926.

Rowland, Benjamin. *The Art and Architecture of India.* Buddhist-Hindu-Jain. London, Penguin Books, 1954.

Seckel, Dietrich. *The Art of Buddhism.* London, Metheun, 1914.

Smith, V.A. *Oxford history of India.* 3rd ed. London, Oxford University Press, 1958.

Stein, Sir Aurel. *The Indo-Iranian Borderlands.* Journal of the Royal Anthropological Institute of Great Britain and Ireland, 1934, Vol. 64.

Subbarao, B. *The Personality of India.* 2nd ed. Baroda, University of Baroda, 1958.

Terra, H.De. and Paterson, T.T. *Studies of the ice-age in India and Associated Human Cultures.* Washington, Carnegie Institute, 1939.

Vats, Madho Sarup. *Excavations at Harappa; Being an account of Archaeological Excavations at Harappa carried out between the years 1920-21 and 1933-34.* In two volumes with plans and plates. Calcutta, Government of India Press, 1940.

Wheeler, R.E.M. *Five Thousand Years of Pakistan; an archaeological outline.* London, Royal India & Pakistan Society, 1950.

Wheeler, R.E.M. *Early India and Pakistan to Ashoka.* New York, Frederick A. Praeger, 1959.

Wheeler, R.E.M. *Pakistan 4,000 years ago.* Pakistan, Miscellany, 1st ed. Karachi, 1952, pp. 21-29.

Wheeler, R.E.M. *The Indus Civilization.* Supplementary volume to the Cambridge History of India, second edition, Cambridge University Press, 1962.

Wheeler, R.E.M. *Rome Beyond the Imperial Frontiers.* London, G. Bell and Sons, 1954.

Index

Egypt, 30.
Ekajata, 167.
Elephant, 30, 113, 122, 125, 127, 136, 139, 170, 173.

F

Faridpur, 177, 179.
Fire temple, 74.
Flint, 24.

G

Gandhara, 22, 67, 69, 71, 89-91, 95, 97, 107, 109, 114, 116, 118-22, 125, 127, 135, 136.
Ganesha, 183.
Ganges, 150.
Ganges Valley, 68.
Garuda, 182.
Gauri, 137.
Ghiasuddin Balban, 127.
Gokul, 162, 163.
Gondopharnes, 125.
Gopala, 152.
Gori, 134.
Govinda Bhita, 162.
Govinda Chandra, 172.
Govinda Swami temple, 177.
Grand Trunk Road, 22.
Grave culture, 67, 68.
Great Bath, 30.
Great Granary, 30.
Graeco-Buddhist, 90.
Greek, 9, 69, 71, 74, 90, 91, 107, 125.
Gujrat, 136.
Gupta, 130, 151, 152, 159, 162, 164, 166, 167, 171, 177, 183, 189.

H

Hammer-stone, 11, 12.
Hand-axe, 11.
Handial, 179.
Harappa, 24, 26, 27, 28, 30, 33, 34, 50, 68.
Hariti, 116, 119, 167.
Harmika, 71, 171.
Harpocrates, 121.
Hathial, 71.
Hayagriva, 167.
Hellenic, 107.
Helios, 125.
Herakles, 125.
Heruka, 167.
Hevajra, 167.
Himalaya, 11, 130, 163.
Hinayana, 95, 119, 166.
Hindu, 125, 129, 134, 136, 139, 151, 152, 159, 166, 174, 182, 189.

Hindu period, 129.
Hindu Shahis, 127.
Hindu Vaishnava, 172.
Hiuen Tsang, 69, 74, 120, 129, 151.
Humped bull, 14.
Huns, 69, 90, 120, 127.
Huvishka, 125.

I

Ice Ages, 11.
India, 71, 97, 151.
Indian Middle Stone Age, 12.
Indo-Greeks, 90.
Indra, 113, 179.
Indrashala Cave, 113.
Indus, 11, 18, 24-26, 28, 33, 34, 51, 67, 68, 125, 129.
Indus Valley, 13, 28, 30, 33, 50, 67, 68.
Iran, 14, 30, 33, 67.
Iranian Plateau, 13, 134.
Iron Age, 67.
Italian Archaeological Mission, 89.

J

Jaina temple, 134.
Jalalabad, 69.
Jalilpur, 22.
Jamalgarhi, 69.
Jambhala, 167.
Jandial, 74.
Japan, 91.
Jarak, 90.
Jaulian, 74.
Java, 164.
Jaykarmanta—Vasaka, 153.
Jesper, 33.
Jessore, 177.
Jewellery, 127.
Jhangar, 28, 50, 53.
Jhelum, 11, 129.
Jhukar, 50, 51, 53.
Jor—Bangla temple, 179.

K

Kabul river, 97.
Kachua, 170.
Kadphises I, 125.
Kafir kot, 130.
Kalachakra, 167.
Kala Nala, 22.
Kalat, 14.
Kali temple, 177.
Kalki, 102.
Kallar Temple, 130.
Kanishka, 12, 69, 74, 89, 95, 118, 125, 127.
Kanishka Relic Casket, 74.

Kanjur stone, 71, 130.
Kantanagar, 177.
Karatoya, 159, 162.
Kartalab Khan, 179.
Kashmir, 129, 130.
Kathiawar, 134.
Khadga, 153, 166.
Khadiravani—Tara, 167, 170.
Khairpur, 24.
Khalia, 177.
Khan Mohammad Mirdha, 179.
Kharoshthi, 71, 74, 89, 122.
Khatvanga, 170.
Khwar, 12.
Khulna, 177.
King priest, 30.
Kodla Math, 177.
Kot Diji, 22, 24, 25, 26, 28, 30.
Kotila Mura, 164, 165, 167.
Krishna, 183.
Kulli, 22.
Kushana, 9, 12, 69, 71, 90, 91, 95, 97, 107, 125, 127.
Kushinagar, 114.
Kuvera, 137, 167.

L

Ladaha Chandra, 172.
Lahore fort, 139.
Lakshmi, 171, 182, 183, 189.
Lakshmi and Archer, 171.
Lalitakara, 170.
Lalmai, 164.
Lapis-lazuli, 20, 128, 183, 189.
Lumbini garden, 113.
Lundi, 71.

M

Mahabharata, 151.
Mahakala, 167.
Mahamaya, 167.
Mahasthangarh, 151, 159-62, 171, 189.
Mahasthavira, 167.
Mahayana, 71, 95, 119, 167, 170.
Mahipala I, 152.
Mainamati, 159, 164, 166, 167, 171, 172, 189.
Mainamati Museum, 170.
Maitreya, 109, 119, 167.
Malakand, 12.
Malot temple, 129.
Manjushri, 167, 170.
Mara, 114, 116.
Mardan, 11, 69, 89.
Marichi, 167.
Marshall, Sir John, 74.
Mathura, 107, 109.

Mathurapur, 177.
Maues, 74, 125.
Mauryan, 69, 91, 125, 127, 151, 159.
Medh, 163.
Mediterranean, 33, 68.
Megalithic, 151.
Meghna, 150.
Mehi, 20.
Menandar, 125.
Mesopotamia, 13, 30, 33.
Micro blades, 26.
Middle East, 9.
Middle Path, 95.
Mingora, 89.
Mirpurkhas, 90, 136.
Mohenjodaro, 28, 30, 33, 34, 50, 90.
Mohra Moradu, 69, 109, 116.
Mongoloid, 33.
Mongoose, 173.
Moro, 90.
Mother Goddess, 33.
Mother of pearl, 33.
Muslim, 26, 134, 139, 154, 162, 174, 177.

N

Nagarjuna, 167.
Nagar Parkar, 136.
Nal, 13, 14, 18.
Naldanga, 177.
Nana, 125.
Nandi bull, 182, 189.
Nataraja, 182.
Navaratna temple, 177.
Neolithic, 22, 24.
Nepal, 113.
Nirvana, 114.
North West Frontier, 9.

O

Oado, 125.
Ora, 89.
Orissa, 177.

P

Pabna, 179.
Padmasambhava, 167.
Paharpur, 152, 159, 163, 166, 171, 173, 183.
Pakistan, 11, 12, 22, 24, 67, 69, 90, 113, 119, 125, 139, 150, 171.
Pala, 152, 158, 159, 162, 165, 166, 170.
Palaeolithic, 11.
Panchika, 116, 119.
Pan-na-fa-tan-na, 151.
Parashurama, 182.

Parkho darra, 12.
Parnashavari, 167, 170.
Parthian, 90, 118, 119, 125, 138.
Parvati, 183.
Pathans, 107.
Pattikera, 158, 170.
Peacock, 25, 34, 139.
Persian, 90, 125.
Peshawar, 69, 74, 90.
Peshawar Museum, 74, 89, 118.
Peshawar University, 12.
Phyllite, 11.
Pipal leaf, 25, 33.
Pir Panjal, 11.
Poonch, 11.
Po-shi-po, 151.
Potwar, 11, 12.
Prajnaparamita, 167.
Pran Nath, Maharaja, 177.
Priya-Darshi, 122.
Proto Austroloid, 33.
Proto Europoid, 68.
Pundra, 151.
Pundravardhana—Bhukti, 150, 151.
Punjab, 125.
Puranic, 177.
Purna Chandra, 172.
Putia, 177.

Q

Quartz, 12.
Quartzite, 33.
Queen Maya, 133.
Quetta, 14.

R

Radha, 183.
Rajaram temple, 179.
Rajhansa, 173.
Rajmahal, 165.
Rajputana, 134.
Rajshahi, 159, 163, 165, 167, 170, 177.
Rama, 182.
Ramayana, 151.
Rana Ghundai, 14.
Ratnasambhaba, 167.
Rawalpindi, 11.
Rhinoceros, 30, 33.
Rig Veda, 69.
Roman, 90, 107.
Romano-Buddhist, 90.

S

Saka, 74, 90.
Shakyamuni, 95, 119.
Salban Vihara, 164, 165, 172.

Salt range, 11, 129.
Samatata, 150, 151, 153, 154, 159, 165, 166, 189.
Samudragupta, 189.
Sanchi, 71.
Sangha, 165.
Sanghao, 11, 12.
Sanghar, 136.
Sanskrit, 67.
Sapta Sindhu, 68.
Sarai Khola, 22, 24.
Sarasvati, 182, 183.
Sarkar Math, 177.
Sarvani, 170.
Sassanian 127, 139.
Schist, 11, 12, 89, 91, 119.
Scythian, 125, 139.
Scytho-Parthians, 69, 74, 90.
Seistan, 125.
Selene, 125.
Sena, 153, 182.
Shahbazgarhi, 89.
Shahi-Tump, 18.
Shahji-ki-Dheri, 74.
Shaikhan-Dheri, 90, 120, 122.
Shakti, 167, 170, 182.
Shala tree, 113, 114.
Shanti Deva, 172.
Shashanka, 189.
Shikhara, 130, 177.
Shiva, 125, 179, 182, 189.
Shaivism, 182.
Shiva lingam, 139.
Shiva temple, 136.
Shri Bhavadeva, 171.
Shri Chandra, 172.
Shri Vasudeva, 172.
Shuddhodana, 113.
Shyama-Tara, 167, 170.
Siddhartha, 113.
Sind, 14, 129.
Singhapura, 129.
Sirkap, 71, 74, 122.
Sirsukh, 71.
Soan, 11.
Somapura, 163, 171.
Song-Yun, 89.
Stone Age, 11-13.
Strato-I, 125.
Sudheran-jo-dharo, 90.
Sumer, 30.
Sumerian, 30.
Sun, 25, 74, 170.
Sun flower, 139.
Sunga, 189.
Surya, 179, 182.
Susa, 14.
Suvarna Chandra, 172.
Swat, 67, 69, 89, 90.
Swat river, 11.

Sylhet, 151.

T

Takht-i-Bahi, 71, 74, 89.
Takshasila, 74.
Tal-i-Bakun, 14.
Talo, 89.
Tando Mohammad Khan, 90.
Tantric cult, 166.
Tara, 167.
Taranath, 152.
Taxila, 22, 69, 71, 74, 109, 116, 120, 122, 125, 127, 137, 139.
Taxila Museum, 113.
Tharelli, 89.
Thar-Parkar, 134, 136, 137.
Three jewels, 114.
Thul Mir Rukan, 90.
Tibet, 97.
Tiger, 30, 33.
Tiger (horned), 33.
Toilet articles, 122.
Trailokya Chandra, 172.
Tripura, Maharaja of, 179.
Tri-ratna, 113, 170, 173.

U

Udegram, 89, 90.

Udyana, 89.
Unicorn, 33.
Ur, 30.
Urna, 109.
Ushnisha, 109.

V

Vairochana, 167.
Vaishnava temple, 136.
Vaishnavi, 182.
Vaishnavite, 154.
Vajra, 113.
Vajrapani, 113, 116.
Vajrasattva, 167.
Vajra Tara, 170.
Valabhatta, 189.
Vanga, 150.
Varendra, 152, 159.
Varman, 154, 182.
Vasudeva, 127.
Vasu Vihara, 151.
Vedas, 135, 136.
Vedic, 179.
Vikrampur, 154, 172.
Vinaya Text, 158.
Vira Deva, 172.
Viradhara Deva, 172.
Virawah, 134, 136.
Vishnu, 136, 137, 172, 179, 182, 183, 189.

Vitapala, 152, 166.

W

Waziri, 107.
West Pakistan, 11, 24, 90, 125, 129, 136.
Western Asia, 107, 119.
Wheel of Law, 113, 114, 116.
White Huns, see Huns
Wild boar, 173.
Writing material, 122.

Y

Yab-yum, 170.
Yaksha, 116, 167.
Yakshi, 116.
Yama, 167.
Yamapukur-Brata, 139.
Yamuna, 183.
Yashodhara, 113.
Yoni, 139.

Z

Zhob culture, 13.
Zoroastrians, 34, 74.